With
Grace AND Grit

With
Grace AND Grit

Life Stories of
John & Eileen Landis

John Landis and Eileen Landis

with Jean Kilheffer Hess

StoryShare, LLC
givestoryshare@gmail.com

Cover and interior design by Beth Oberholtzer

ISBN 978-0-9832977-8-9

Contents

Acknowledgements

God has been good to us and has met us in the events of our lives. He has met our needs with blessings in abundance.

We thank our children for encouragement and support. We couldn't have done all we did without their journey with us.

We are grateful for both sets of parents who taught us and helped us to be who we are.

I, John, give special credit to my wife and companion, Eileen, for all she is as wife, companion, and helper through all the events of life we faced together.

We have received much from our friends who have walked with us in our journey.

Our prayer is that all who read this story will be encouraged and blessed.

We thank Darryl, our son, for his encouragement to record our memories and his diligent help in editing this book.

We thank Jean Kilheffer Hess, who has been a blessing in helping to write our story.

The Families and Faith That Formed Us

John's Story

Each family has its own culture. I saw this growing up when we'd visit with Mom's family or Pop's family.

My mother, Ruth Frey Garman, came from a family that loved to have fun. The Garmans were fun-loving, party-going: a lot of meals, hot dog roasts, corn roasts, that kind of thing. Even though Grandpa, Frank Garman, was a pastor, he liked joking and just having a good time.

Pop's family felt that kind of stuff was improper, I guess. The Landises were more proper. Pop's parents, Anna Mary Oberholtzer and John L. Landis, were more dignified, formal. They talked about family, farming, money, and church.

The Landises were wealthy, had property; the Garmans were hired people who were in a lot lower echelon of finances. There was a big difference between them.

I'm not exactly sure why Pop and Mom got together. I don't remember that story; I don't know if I ever heard it. I know how Grandma Landis got Grandpa Landis to date her: it was through a box social, and she set it up that he would buy her lunch box. That got them started, and they were soon married.

The Garmans were tall people, more thin, hard-working. The Oberholtzers and Landises were more stocky. Grandpa Landis had a stout, rotund, five-and-a-half-foot frame. Grandma Landis was petite and less than five feet in height.

The families were just different, and it carried down to the uncles and aunts. I think there was only one other Mennonite on my mom's side. She had seven

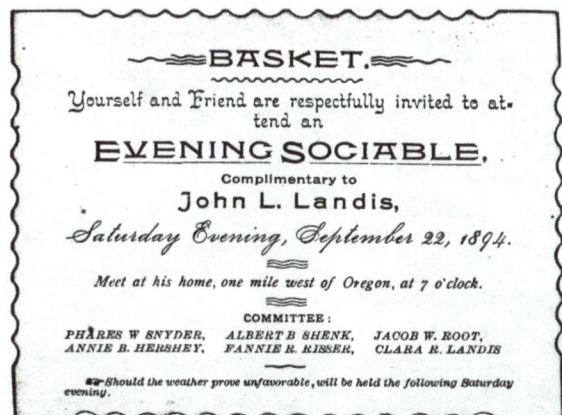

Invitation to the box social where John's grandparents, Anna Mary Oberholtzer and John L. Landis, started dating.

John's mother, Ruth Garman's, family of origin. Left to right: Ruth, her father, Frank, siblings Roy, Esther, Mary, and her mother, Katie Frey Garman holding Frank.

John's paternal grandparents John L. and Anna Mary Oberholtzer Landis, 1942. They are at their beef cattle and tobacco farm on Oregon Pike, Lancaster.

John's paternal grandfather John L. Landis, was born in 1873 and is about 20 years old here.

brothers and sisters. But on my dad's side, everybody was Mennonite, and everybody was a conservative and followed the rules and regulations. Not so much on the Garman side.

That made a very good combination when Pop and Mom had children. We had both sides genetically. When it came to having fun, we could have fun. Mom, she was for having company and doing things and going places. And Pop, he was more "Let's just sit and talk about things." I enjoyed both sides.

My grandmas were both strong women. I always said that the men did not have charge—on the Garman side nor on the Landis side. My Grandma Garman, when it was something she wanted, she just said it. She didn't play games with Grandpa. She'd say "Let's go . . . ," "Let's get . . . ," "Let's do . . ." whatever. Grandpa never questioned her.

On the Landis side, my Grandma Landis, who was an Oberholtzer, she's the one who had the most money when they got married. If I may say this, she kind of had the rule of the checkbook. I know Pop borrowed money from Grandpa Landis to buy things. I can remember that, from right after the Depression and from World War II. But Grandma's the one that held the money. That was an interesting thing to me.

Mom had some of her mother's approach. We children talked about that, how did Mom control Pop and the pocketbook? We're not quite sure how she did that.

John's maternal grandmother Katie Frey Garman (1888–1979), about 1904.

John's paternal grandmother Anna Mary Oberholtzer Landis (1876–1962), right, circa 1890.

If she wanted something, she got it. Mom was the one that pretty much gave me the training and direction on how to act, how to behave, how to spend my money. Pop didn't have much to say about it, but Mom did.

I never heard them argue, never heard them get angry about something they wanted or didn't want. But she would never say that I could borrow money to get something. She'd always say, "Go ask your dad." I knew they talked about it. When did they do that? I don't know. They apparently had a time and a place, because they didn't do it in front of us children when they talked it out. Often puzzled me, often wondered.

Mom was a conversationalist. And I had a different role than any of the other children. The others pretty much agree with that I think. When we'd be pulling weeds she'd, in a conversation, talk about, "What do you think about the way you drive your car, John?" Because I bought a new car—a new Ford—when I was 18 years old. Or church things. She would— again in conversation while doing something: picking peas, shelling peas, pulling weeds, doing something in the kitchen (I helped a lot in the kitchen, too, even though I had four sisters)—she did it by conversation.

John's mother Ruth Garman Landis at home in the late 1960s. She is on the phone in the dining room of the East Petersburg farm on Graystone Road. This farm was later purchased and demolished by the adjacent quarry.

Mom was the one that said what she thought about my girlfriends. I didn't have many girlfriends, but she left me know what she thought about them.

Pop did too, but Pop was different in his approach. He used to say, "Nothing good'll come out of Lebanon County." Mom, she was just interested in the girl and knowing what she was like.

Mom loved flowers. Mom loved to bake. All that stuff is part of me too.

They could speak Pennsylvania Dutch—both of them—and there was an awful lot of PA Dutch flying. I got to the point where I could pretty near understand it, but then I left home and I lost all I had ever known.

I can remember when I was 16, Mom said, "We're going to town today, and I'm going to teach you how to treat a lady." We walked out to our '49 Buick, and she stood outside the car. I said, "Come on, Mom!" and she said, "You gotta open that door for me." I got out, went around the car, opened the door, and let her in.

We drove into Lancaster, and I parked on East King Street. I'll never forget this. I got out of the car, and went to the sidewalk, and Mom stayed sitting in the car. (Oh yeah, yeah, yeah, come on, think.) So I opened the door for her and left her get out.

She wanted to hold my arm. She said, "No, you gotta be on the other side of me. The man always walks toward the street side." We spent that whole day in Lancaster shopping. We bought things that she wanted, but she took me along and told me what to do and how to do it. She said, "I want you to remember that: always treat a lady like a lady."

My brothers didn't get that kind of training; why did I have to have it? I needed it, I guess. It stuck, too.

John's mother Ruth enjoyed growing flowers. She stands in her garden behind the East Petersburg farmhouse. John shares a love of flowers and carries on her tradition with flowers shown growing here on the farm he and Eileen purchased from the Ebersoles (middle) and at their Thompson Avenue home near Annville (below).

Mom was firm. She meant what she said. I don't recall of her yelling at me at all or even my siblings. She would take it as a yes or no, this is what you do, and you knew that you were going to do it.

Pop, he was quicker of temper. He spanked. I had a couple pretty good spankings. Probably deserved them, I don't know. He did the spanking, and he could yell.

Pop was a hard-working fellow. He was known in the neighborhood for his ability to work: to spear tobacco, for instance, cut tobacco, pick potatoes. We had 25–30 acres of potatoes and 12–15 acres of tobacco. And he knew how to challenge. Different times, starting when I was about 14, he'd say, "I'll know you're a man when you can beat me at working." When I was 16, I did! Surprised him. I had a lot of fire in my bones, too, I guess, but I was determined that I was going to earn that.

John's parents, Ruth Garman Landis and Elam Landis. Wedding anniversary photo, unknown year, taken in the basement of their home next to Root's Nursery off Route 72. Note Elam's customary bowtie with the plain suit.

He would challenge me when we'd be working on a piece of equipment. I was always learning. I had my nose in everything that he wanted to do. He would say, "What do you think about how we're going to repair this? What are we going to do here?" He would accept my opinion. He was a good teacher in that sense of helping me to do mechanical work because he didn't like to call a mechanic in to fix something.

He bought a welder—I was probably about 14 when he bought the first welding machine—and he wanted me to learn. He said, "You'd make a good welder." That's all he said. He said, "This is how you do it." He didn't know that much about it himself.

So he took Mark and I to an evening school to learn welding. Pop was—for all of his quickness, all of his opinions—he had a good side to him that wanted his children to be the best and do the best. May not have agreed with him, but he still wanted you to make that decision that said, "I think this is the best way to do it."

I remember a time that I was supposed to disc the cornfield. We had a pretty long lane. He had about four foot where he had grass growing alongside the lane and the field. I was probably 12, 13 years old. I thought, why in the world do we waste all that ground? I'm going to disc that in with the rest of the field.

I can remember he came home and he walked out to the field. He said, "What are you trying to do with this sod along the lane?" I said, "Why don't we farm it? Grow some crops on it." He said, "Do you know why I have that grass there?" I said, "No." He said, "Think." Then it dawned on me that we had our telephone line laid in that grass. It was down probably about a foot. He said, "There's a telephone wire, remember that?" "Yeah, that's right."

John's father Elam Landis, July 4, 1976. He always said if the corn was knee-high by July 4, it would be a good crop. This was a very good year for corn!

John's father attended Lancaster Business College. It was $12 per month for tuition.

"Now this is going to rain, and that dirt is going to wash out on the lane. Are you ready to shovel all that dirt back up in the field?" No, I wasn't! Then he said, "Maybe you better figure out a way how, if it rains, that the water doesn't wash the dirt out into the lane." So I dug a little furrow the whole way out the lane. That was hard work. But it kept the soil pretty much in the field. That's the way Pop taught me. I learned.

He also liked to play games like checkers that required good thinking and trying to figure out ahead of time what your moves were going to be, because you couldn't recover if you made the wrong move. He'd tell me that, he'd say, "Now are you ready to go?" I'd say, "Yeah." "Are you sure you want to go the way you think you're going to go?" He'd challenge that way. "Are you sure you want to do that?" He did that the whole way up my life.

When I was farming, I could go to the bank—I had established good credit with the bank—I could go to the bank and borrow money without any signatures. I can still see him looking at me and saying, "Are you sure you want to have that kind of resource that you won't overextend yourself and borrow too much money? Banks want to lend money. If they think somebody's going to pay them back, they'll lend more and more and more, and I don't want you to get caught. So, are you sure?"

That always made me think when I borrowed money. And helped me a lot when I got a lot bigger on my farming operation. Having a standing opportunity at the bank to borrow any amount of money to pay for fertilizer and chemicals and seeds and other stuff. "Are you sure?" is always in the back of my head.

It still is today when it comes to making decisions in leadership—which I don't do much anymore—but I did that over the time of being very active in the church. "Are you sure? Have you thought that through?" That's a very key component to me of knowing what to do and what not to do. I think that kept me from doing some things. I could have made some bad moves because I wasn't sure.

Here's what I mean: in 1955 when I wasn't married yet and still lived at home, I did my first year of farming. I rented some ground and put potatoes out, tobacco.

'55 was a dry year. I barely got all my money back. That taught me a big lesson. So yeah, "Are you sure?" That was something that still hangs on my mind.

• • • • •

In our family growing up, two things seemed most important. One was our spiritual life. Mom and Pop wanted us to grow up to be good Mennonites, good Christians. Am I willing to give myself as a Christian to the church, do what the church wanted? The second was safety, and I'll get to that a bit later.

Elam Landis relaxing and reading.

We went to Landis Valley Mennonite Church, and when I think about my spiritual formation the first thing I think about is the elderly ladies at Landis Valley. I can see them sitting on the first two to three benches on the women's side, up in the amen corner. They also taught the little children in the classroom back of the pulpit. This was a group of 20-some women that traded off in teaching. They took such an interest in me. I don't know if they pitied Mom or if they just loved us. I'd like to think they just loved us.

I can remember the teachers picking me up and setting me on the bench for class. There were full-sized benches up there—they didn't have children's benches or chairs. It was called the "card class." Every Sunday you had a card, about two inches wide and three inches long, with a picture on the one side and the scripture verse and story on the other side. I still have some of them cards.

You got blue tickets for verses you learned. After you had ten or fifteen verses, you traded your little blue tickets in and got a red ticket. That would get you a Bible or a Testament or another book.

I always liked to read. I had a whole bunch of Be story books. Be Kind. Be Loving. All kinds of Be's like that. Had a little story and pictures with it. That impacted me.

Something else that really impressed me was my dad was strict on having morning devotions with the family. We'd sit in the kitchen in a circle. When we were old enough to read, he would have us read the passage of scripture.

Pop was a good reader. He knew how to spell, and he was good at that kind of stuff. So when we got to all these long words in the Old Testament, he would stop us and say, "This is how you say that word." He'd break it down into the sections of the word and have you say it, right in the midst of the devotional. He'd insist.

Even if you only got one verse read, that was good enough if you got it read correctly. That left an impression on me. It turned some of my siblings off, but it

Before they call, I will answer; and while they are yet speaking, I will hear.—ISA. 65:24.

The goodness of God endureth continually.—PSA. 52:1.

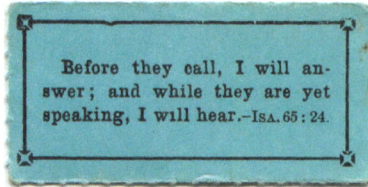

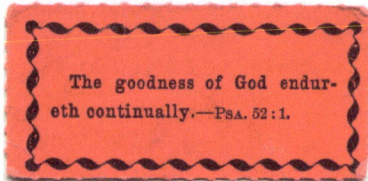

Blue tickets and red tickets, used in Sunday School to keep track of students' progress in memorizing Scripture. Red tickets could be redeemed for a prize.

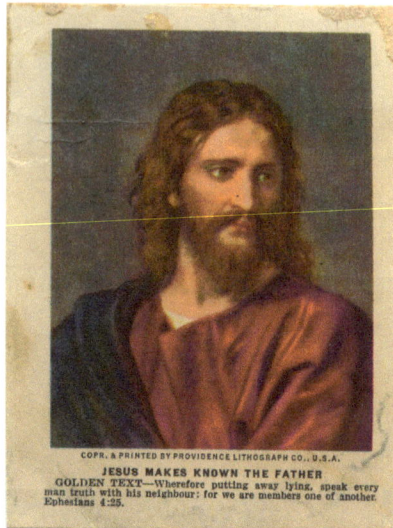

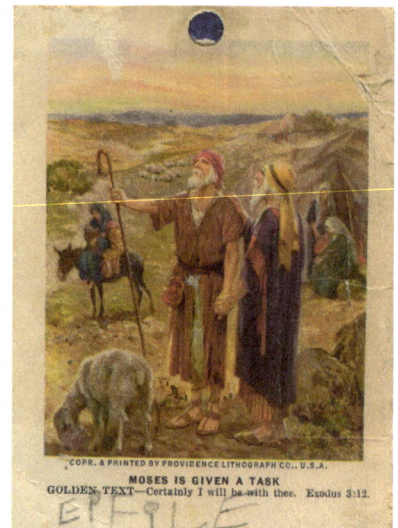

JESUS MAKES KNOWN THE FATHER
GOLDEN TEXT—Wherefore putting away lying, speak every man truth with his neighbour; for we are members one of another. Ephesians 4:25.

MOSES IS GIVEN A TASK
GOLDEN TEXT—Certainly I will be with thee. Exodus 3:12.

Primary students received these cards. One side had a picture and caption, and the other side had the Bible story printed on it. Cards here dated July 1943.

didn't turn me off because I knew that back of every one of those words, there was not only a Bible story but was a correct way of saying another language.

Of course my mother read to us from Ergermeier's storybook. That used to be a very good children's Bible story book. She read a lot of stories out of there to us children. I have a copy that I got from a dear saint at Gingrichs because I had worn the other one out. The covers were gone; it was really in bad shape.

Another person who left an impression was my Grandpa Garman, who was a preacher. He took a keen interest in me. As soon as I could drive, my mom had me driving Grandpa. He had a lot of revival meetings, tent meetings, and she had me drive him to those meetings. Grandpa always studied and talked when we went to the meeting. He was full of fun afterwards, but on the way there he was concentrating on what he was going to preach that night.

Fact is, I received Christ as my Savior at North End, which doesn't exist any more. That's where I received Christ, at Grandpa's preaching. He was a storyteller. When he preached, he illustrated what he wanted to say through stories. That impacted me a lot. That's the way I generally did when I was preaching a lot. Not many of us are black and white or logical/illogical thinkers, we think in story form. I still do a lot of that when I teach or preach; I use a lot of stories.

Those dear ladies that I talked about, 20-some ladies, they wanted me to stay at Landis Valley when I got married. They came to me and told me that they will pray for me. I believe they did. I believe some of the things in my life happened because of those ladies and their prayers. They're no longer here, but God still honors the prayers of those dear saints. I think it's a beautiful thing.

I know that when I became a pastor, was ordained, every one of those ladies that was still living gave me a note—through Mom—that they were still praying for me and they were going to continue to pray for me as a pastor. So as every one of those died, I felt like I was losing something. Wow.

Growing up, a typical Sunday morning service included a lot of singing. We'd go to Sunday school, come back from Sunday school, and children up to about 12 years of age would sit in the front benches. Landis Valley at that time had probably 300-some people attending. It was a fairly large church.

Landis Valley Mennonite Church, where John grew up attending. It is located at 2420 Kissel Hill Road, Lancaster, PA.

The superintendent would ask the classes, starting with the nursery class, "What did you learn today in Bible verses? Do you have the Bible verse you can say?" Usually, they did. They went down through all the classes through age 12, and he would ask specific questions. The teachers always had the pupils ready.

After that was singing. We'd have maybe three songs. We were good four-part singers at Landis Valley, we didn't just sing the melody. Once a month, because Ira Landis was one of the pastors—he was into German; he could speak German and read and write German—he asked to have one or two songs sung in German.

One of my grandma's brothers, Christ Oberholtzer, had every song in probably three or four songbooks memorized. He was a big man, well-built and about six feet three inches tall. He was a school teacher, a music teacher, and he'd lead the German song. We sang them. It was something that I have a warm feel in my heart about. It was beautiful.

My brother Mark and I both led singing at Landis Valley. The pastor would ask to have a certain song sung. Neither of our pastors could sing the bottom of a barrel. They would pick out the song, and that's when I liked those dear elderly ladies up front, too. It wasn't many songs that those ladies didn't know. Mark wondered how I'd get those songs going, I said, "Because I trust those older ladies. They'll help you lead that song." And they would. We'd have those three songs and, like I said, the song the pastor wanted.

Next somebody had devotions. Then we had the pastor stand up and generally preach. Ira preached longer than Levi did. Levi thought the 30-minute sermon was long enough. But Ira would preach three quarters to a full hour. Now Ira was the fellow that was educated; he had graduated from Penn State and taken some other seminary courses. But he preached long sometimes.

We had a lot of visiting speakers in. Missions was a big thing, and our church had a lot of missionaries. Some of the missionary speakers were on furlough or just

John's family at Uncle Eli Humbert's home in Ironville, PA, circa 1949. Left to right, standing: Ruth, Miriam, Mark, John, Elizabeth; Left to right, seated: John's mother Ruth, Rhoda, John's Pop Elam holding James.

going to be sent out to the field. We had several ladies who were nurses and missionaries who went to Tanganyika (Tanzania). One of them was Lois Landis, Preacher Ira Landis' daughter.

After the sermon, we'd stand around and talk. Us boys would go out and look at the cars. I don't know why boys had such an interest in that, but we did. Some of those cars were pretty high end: LaSalles, Cadillacs. Landis Valley was more or less a rich Mennonite congregation. These men had beautiful big cars. Wow, would I love to have some of them now! Oh my!

Usually we went to somebody's place for lunch after church.

The second most important thing taught in our family was safety. Both Pop and Mom wanted us to be safe. Accidents, injuries were very critical to them. That's because they loved us so much. Sometimes I had to wonder did they love us too much, but I don't think so.

I think of a time when I was a boy, when my sister Ruth was probably three years old, and I was five or six. We were sitting on a tractor seat underneath where the hay fork would go up, and then you could take it over to the hay mow and drop the load of hay down to the hay mow. The hired man did something wrong, and that fork dropped down when it wasn't supposed to. It missed me but hit my sister Ruth, who was sitting on the tractor seat. It went right past her head and hit her in the leg.

I can still see my Pop. From the overhead log at the top of the mow, he made one jump to the wagon, and then down to the floor and over to pick Ruth up. He told me to "run in to Mom and get rags, clean rags," because she was bleeding pretty bad.

Safety is something that Pop always tried to teach us, whether it was driving or working with equipment. And I don't know about the other boys, Mark or James, but he taught me that I'm a protector of women. "You're a brother to your sisters, you're a son of your mother, you are a male, and you are a protector." That's ingrained in me still today. Safety, that's very precious.

Eileen's Story

My mother's mother, Margaret Wenger Kreider, we did not see very often because she lived in Kinzers, and we lived up here in Lebanon County. In those days you didn't travel every week. You didn't use the phone, for that far away, unless you had an emergency. But I do have some good memories of her.

Eileen's maternal grand-
mother Margaret L.
"Maggie" Wenger, as a girl,
about 1900.

Margaret Wenger and
Willis Groff Kreider
wedding photo. They
married May 30, 1903
in Kinzers, PA.

Eileen's grandparents,
Margaret and Willis
Kreider, circa early
1940s, on their farm
off Route 30 in Kinzers
area.

My mother's father, Willis Groff Kreider, died when I was about seven, so I don't remember much of him because of the distance. I understand he was a farmer and a school teacher. His older sister made him a book bag that he put over the horse's back to carry his school books in, and he rode horseback to teach school. Later he got a covered wagon pulled by two horses, and he'd take his own children and neighborhood children along to the Gap school. Around 1910 he bought a farm near Kinzers, Pennsylvania, and he raised produce and sold it at market.

Grandpa was one of the first farmers in the neighborhood to have electricity. And he worked with six or eight neighbors to bring telephone lines into their farm community. When they finished with the job, they had a chicken corn soup supper to celebrate.

Grandpa and Grandma did many family activities with their children such as sled-dings, having picnics in the woods, or playing croquet games after the day's work was done. Grandma played the organ, Grandpa was a good singer, and the family would sing together. Maybe my grandparents passed on to me the enjoyment of playing games and having family fun together.

I have pictures where Grandma Kreider took us down to Wilmington, Delaware, on a boat ride. We always went to Holloway Beach as an extended family and spent the day swimming. There were eight in my mother's family; it was quite a crew. We didn't have swim suits, so we all rented swim suits for the day. That was a good time.

Every year at July Fourth, Grandma had a picnic—a corn roast they called it—in her front yard, which we were invited to. And we spent time with them every year at Christmas. So those two times each year stand out to me.

Grandpa Willis Kreider and daughters: Eileen's mother Elizabeth on his shoulders and her sister Arlene in his arms, at their farm in Kinzers, circa 1926.

The Kreider family enjoying their annual summer trip to Holloway Beach (no longer exists) on the Chesapeake Bay, Maryland. Left to right: Aunt Mary Kreider, Grandma Maggie, Elizabeth Kreider, Cousin Wilbur Hershey, Irvin Kreider, Uncle Earl and Aunt Margaret Denlinger behind cousin Dawn Kreider, Mother Elizabeth behind Eileen and cousin Anna Marie Kreider, Aunt Katherine Hershey behind cousin Betty Denlinger and cousin Jeanette Hershey, Father Jacob holding Virginia on his shoulders behind Uncle Frank Hershey and cousin Glen Hershey.

Grandma Kreider had an annual corn roast on July 4 at their farm in Kinzers, here about 1940.

Grandma was a small, short lady. She was a kind person but more or less quiet. I don't remember having long conversations with her or anything like that. In fact, when we would go see her, there were so many cousins around that I related more to my cousins than what I did to her. But she was there. I think we were down there a couple times that we stayed overnight, too.

Eileen's paternal grandfather E. Dervin "Pappy" Hart, born August 2, 1879, at age 17 in an unknown location in Juniata County, PA.

Eileen's paternal grandmother, "Grammy" Annie Benner Hart, born August 18, 1880, at about age 15. Location unknown.

My grandparents on my dad's side, Annie Benner Hart and E. Dervin Hart, lived close by us for a while when I was growing up, so I got to see them more. We called them Pappy and Grammy. We always said Pappy had selective hearing because he would not hear what Grammy was saying, but if anyone else would talk to him in that tone of voice, why, he could hear!

I thought of Pappy as a kind person. More or less quiet, a nice person. He always had pink lozengers, and we could go to him after church and get some. We liked that. I remember staying at their place different times, and we always had big sugar cookies for breakfast. I have good memories of Grammy and Pappy.

What I got from my uncle and my dad and so forth, was that when Grammy was younger, she had mental problems. Sometimes when she was not feeling good, she would throw things at Pappy. Evidently she must have had post-partum depression after at least one of her children. My dad's older sisters would take their eight-month-old sister, Ruth, along to school with them, because they were afraid of what Grammy might do to Ruth while they were at school.

Dervin and Annie Hart, Eileen's grandparents, on their farm near Quentin on Route 322 where Eileen grew up, circa 1940s.

Eileen's mother Elizabeth Kreider, born April 19, 1914, in striped stockings third from left, with her school friends at a Kinzers, PA area farm, circa early 1930s.

Grammy and Pappy lived in Juniata County near her parents. Grammy's dad made Pappy promise that he'd never put her away in a mental institution, so he just lived with the circumstances. She would go out into the woods, and he didn't know where she was, and he'd have to go find her and persuade her to come back home. When she was older—when I knew her—she was a kind person, a loving person. There was none of that in her then.

My mother, Mary Elizabeth Kreider, was one of eight children—four boys and four girls. Her dad and brothers called her Johnnie when she was little because she loved being outside with her dad. One day she told her dad she wasn't going to answer unless he called her Elizabeth. At the dinner table he asked her three times to do something, using the name Johnnie. Finally he said, "Alright, no one should call her Johnnie anymore." Some tried calling her Lizzie, but the only name she would answer to was Elizabeth.

My parents, Elizabeth Kreider and Jacob Hart, were married June 20, 1934. She was 20 and worked at the Hershey Garment Factory before they were married, making about $8 a week. He was farming with his father, and neither of them had much money saved. They received a set of silverware from her parents, and her aunt, Mina Kreider, gave them a set of china. Elizabeth's mother continued to add to the china set until they had twelve settings. Mother gave this set of china to me.

Eileen's parents, Elizabeth Kreider Hart and Jacob Hart. This is a professional photo taken at Moseman's Photography in Manheim, PA on Elizabeth & Jacob's 25th wedding anniversary. The couple was not able to afford photography at their June 20, 1934 wedding.

Jacob and Elizabeth's first home was two rooms in her parent's house on the Kreider farm near Kinzers in Lancaster County. Her parents were ready to retire, so they decided to "farm on the shares" together. "Farming on the shares" meant that the owner of the farm would share in the expenses and income of the crops, and the farmer would do the work of planting and harvesting. Usually the farmer owned any animals on the farm.

Mother's dad asked how many cows they planned to buy, and Daddy said he planned to buy twelve cows. But Daddy worked one day a week for Bill Moyer, a cow dealer, and Bill helped him buy more cows. Soon the herd numbered twenty-one cows he milked by hand. His father-in-law was not too happy about the increased herd. Daddy was using more feed for his cattle, which decreased the share money Elizabeth's parents were getting from the farm. Mother and Daddy decided they needed to find a farm of their own to keep good relationships with her parents.

My dad's brother, Uncle Clair, was farming in Lebanon County, and my parents went to visit him and Aunt Mabel to ask if they knew of any farms for rent. Uncle Clair told them about a 100 acre farm for rent not far away, on Route 322 just west of Quentin. They went to see the farm and to talk with Mr. Eby, the owner. They rented the farm that same day. My parents moved there a few weeks later, in the spring of 1935.

The farm had a beautiful, big stone house with eleven rooms. Mother and Daddy only had enough furniture for three rooms. The house didn't have a furnace or an indoor bathroom, and during the first few years the only water available was from the well at the barn. All the water used in the house had to be carried in from the barn. They didn't have money, at first, to buy a washing machine or refrigerator. So Mother washed their clothes on a scrubbing board, which was hard work, and Daddy sometimes helped her. They carried their food to the cellar to keep it cool.

Eileen Hart as a young child, about 1940. She was born May 2, 1937.

Eileen and her sister, Virginia, playing together at their parents' first farm along Route 322 near Quentin, PA.

Eileen's family of origin. Left to right: Eileen, Elizabeth Kreider Hart, baby Dervin, Jacob Hart, and Virginia.

Home farm where Eileen spent most of her childhood (she moved there at 10), on Starner Road west of Quentin in Lebanon County, PA.

Mother and Daddy lived on this farm from 1935 until 1947. I was born two years after they moved there, in 1937. The upstairs was cold in winter as there was no heat in the upstairs bedrooms. We had a summer kitchen, with covered porch between the main house and the summer kitchen. They used the summer kitchen at butchering times and for storage.

I was the oldest child in the family, and I had a happy childhood. I have a sister four years younger than me, a brother two years younger than her, then a younger sister. We had a sister in between me and my next sister, but she only lived three weeks. I was only two, so I don't remember her at all.

Also when I was two: we lived right along 322, and one day a truck driver came in and said to my mother, "Do you know where your daughter is?" Here I was sitting in the center of 322, just sitting there! There was no traffic like there is now.

Farms then had lots of buildings outside, and one of the small buildings became our playhouse. It had a small table with chairs, and an old, two-burner kerosene stove that didn't work anymore for us to play with. My sister and I spent many hours playing house.

We played and we had fun. I remember playing paper dolls. Our parents played board games and outside games with us. Daddy would play checkers with me game after game. I would always cry when he beat me, which he usually did. He would say, "We can stop playing," and I would say, as I was crying, "I want to play another game."

We worked too. I remember having to do dishes. My sister and I would stack up chairs from the sink—I always washed (I still like to wash dishes, not dry)—and around

to the cupboard where they went in. I stood on a stool because I was a little bigger than her, and she stood on the chairs to dry the dishes and put them away. I wonder how my mother had patience with us, because we didn't particularly like the job. Sometimes it would sit there a while before we got to it, but we did it.

I was my parents' first child, and my mother was ill during most of my growing up years. The doctor didn't know what was the matter with her. She sort of drug her one leg and foot when she walked, and she walked that way for quite a few years. In the house she would go from table to chairs, holding on to them as she walked. My dad always helped her to walk when they were in public.

Eileen remembers lots of fun times as a child, here swimming in a trough with her siblings and cousin on her family's farm near Quentin, PA. Left to right: Virginia, Anna Marie Kreider, Dervin, Eileen. About 1945.

She became very ill when I was 15, and they finally sent her to a hospital in Philadelphia. My dad took her down. I think she spent a couple days there. After they came home, the doctor told my dad that she won't live more than a couple months or something like that.

They had an anointing service, and my sister and I were in the room. My sister would have been 11 or 12 at that time. Several of Mother's sisters were there too. I definitely remember of the bishop praying that Mother would live to see her children grow up. Well I was only 15 at the time, but I thought "grow up?" So that was sort of, I don't know what kind of experience for me. Scary in a way.

She lived to be 87, so mother saw her children and grandchildren—all that. In that way, that was a special prayer answered. But she did have to go in a wheelchair eventually; she wasn't healed completely. But we feel at that moment she was healed in a sense because she didn't die right then or when they had expected her to.

Some time later she must have had some sickness that she was sent to Reading hospital. There the doctor diagnosed her as having amyotrophic lateral sclerosis (ALS), the same thing that Lou Gehrig died of. I have the doctor's note that he wrote to her and said that's what it was.

As a result of that, I did a lot of housework, a lot of cooking. I also helped my dad on the farm, did a lot of milking for him. There was one experience that stands out to me during that time. I remember my dad would always call me to get up and help milk. He would be downstairs reading his Bible when I came down, before we went out. I remember at that time he took me on his lap. I was pretty big to sit on his lap. He said, "We'll get through this." We did.

At Reading Hospital they told her if she keeps walking and moving and exercising, it might help her. But then her doctor told her she may as well go to a wheelchair and save her strength and energy. She went in a wheelchair and was on the wheelchair for about 40 years.

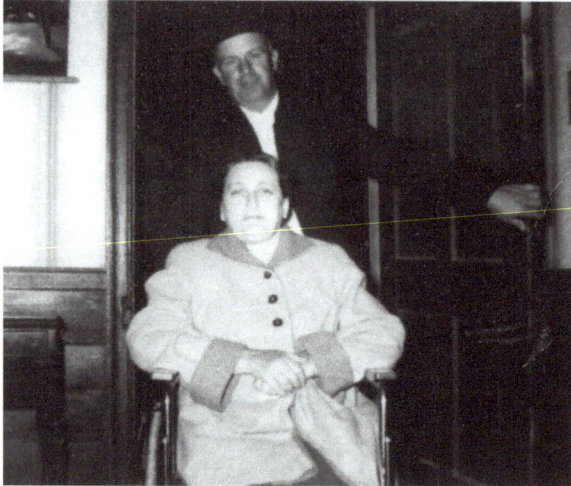

Eileen captioned this photo in a memory book, "Home again! The wheelchair did not keep Mother home. Daddy took Mother along with him often." Here Elizabeth and Jacob return home to their farm on Starner Road in Lebanon County.

Eileen's mother painted this piece of the Starner Road farm, Lebanon County.

One thing—my mother never complained. I never heard her complain. I suppose she did, but I didn't hear her. My dad would often take her away along with him. When I think about it now, that had to be an added effort on his part. That he would take her away when he was going to … well, for anything, for parts or something like that. He would take her along in the car, knowing her need to get out.

She kept busy by sewing for her girls. In her later years she also made many pillow tops and heart-shaped pillows that she gave to her grandchildren and others as gifts. Also in her later years she sewed thousands of sun bonnets that she sold in Lancaster County gift shops.

Eileen on her blue bike as her sister Virginia, looks on. Late 1940s at the Starner Road farm. Eileen kept this bike until after she was married, when a hired man apparently dismantled it to get a part for his own bike.

Even though my mother was sickly, I still had lots of fun as a teen. Whenever I had free time I liked to read. And we had youth activities. I did not have to stay home because of work to be done. My parents made sure of that. I was also allowed to go to Lancaster Mennonite High School (LMH), and I dormed down there Monday through Friday. When I think of that, it was, I'm sure, a sacrifice on my parents' part. We weren't rich but to afford that and also to let me go that I was away from home. I really enjoyed those years at LMH.

• • • • •

What was most important to us? We were a family that went to church a lot. We went to church Sunday morning and Sunday night if there was church. We went to prayer meetings. We were quite involved. My dad was never a minister, but he helped to start the Elm Street Menno- nite Church in the city of Lebanon. It was a small church, probably 40 or 50 people. He and the minister, Sidney Gingrich, did lots of visiting on Saturday afternoons.

Andy Stoessel, pictured fourth from left, was one of the first members of Elm Street Mennonite Church, which began holding Sunday services on October 23, 1955 with 36 people attending. Andy's son, Harold Stoessel, stands next to him behind two of Harold's children. Remaining from left: Elizabeth Hart, Jacob Hart, uniden- tified girl, Carlene Hart. Circa late 1950s.

My dad loved children. My dad was killed in a farming accident before we had any chil- dren. So he never saw any of his grandchildren. But if he would have, he would have loved them to pieces. He would invite people to come out from Lebanon to our farm, and chil- dren—we always had children there. He would let them drive the tractor—well, he would hold them while he was driving tractor. The children just loved him. So I would say family and church were very important to my dad, and to my mother too.

Church started at 9:00 on Sunday mornings. We were almost always on time for that. Sometimes in the evening, because of the cows being milked, we didn't get there on time. It used to frustrate me, especially when I was a teenager, that we had to walk into church late.

On Sunday mornings we had two songs and a short devotional. Then we went to Sunday school till around 10:00. After Sunday school we had a couple songs and then another devotional, which usually the deacon or somebody else read. Never anybody that was not ordained. Then the deacon would sit up front on the bench while the minister would preach. If there was any visiting preacher preaching, then the regular preacher would sit on the bench too.

When the message was done, they always had testimonies to the message by the people on the bench. Each would give a response or sometimes they would just say, "I say amen to the message." Then we had a closing song and a benediction. That was

"Church has been and always will be an important part of my life." —Eileen

> Lebanon Pa
> Feb 17 1946
>
> Dear Eileen
> We wish you the Lords Blessing
> and protection in your young life
> and in time when the Lord
> calls you may give your life
> fully to his will
>
> Father

Note in Eileen's autograph book from her father.

every Sunday. Church has been and always will be an important part of my life.

My early faith and understanding of God was formed by everything combined. Beyond Sunday school and church, we always had family devotions before we left home in the morning: my dad would read the Bible to us. He probably read the Scripture that was in the Sunday school book; they would have listings. He always read it, and then he prayed.

My dad lived his faith, and that helped to form me.

Formal Schooling

Eileen: *I went to public school for the first six grades. Then my dad helped to get a Mennonite school started, called Dohner's Mennonite School, north of Annville. It was a one-room schoolhouse with nine grades. It was all Mennonite children that went there.*

There were no indoor bathrooms at this school. And each day two students would walk about a mile to Henry Stover's home for a pail of drinking water. It was great to get out of class to do that, especially on a nice day.

There was one other fellow in my class, and only one in the seventh grade. I went seventh and eighth. Two students in the ninth grade, two that were just putting in time. They wanted to quit school at 15. They put in time that year. I know the teacher did the best she could during my seventh and eight grades, but I felt like I did not learn very much those two years.

Anyway, I went from there with one classmate, that was in school just because he had to be, to ninth grade at Lancaster Mennonite High School where I had 70-some-plus in my class. That was an adjustment. I was determined that I'm going to do good down there. I studied like crazy. I managed to stay near the top of my class.

But we had fun in the dorm! Of course it was very much more structured than it is now. One night we were all hanging out the windows and passing things from the upstairs to downstairs, and we got caught. I don't know what we were passing. Just notes or whatever.

We were told 7:00 to 9:15 was study time. You weren't supposed to be in anyone else's room unless you had permission. Well, lots of different times we got caught being in somebody else's room. One of my friends roomed with a girl who was really tall. She was in somebody's room and didn't belong in there. We heard the matron coming, and so she knelt behind the bed but she was so tall, her

Drawing Eileen made of Dohner's Mennonite School when she attended there during seventh and eighth grade, circa 1950.

Friends waiting for the ride home on Friday afternoon at LMS dorm, circa 1952. Left to right: Barbara Lamp, Nora Beiler, unidentified, Alice Herr.

Eileen's high school senior portrait.

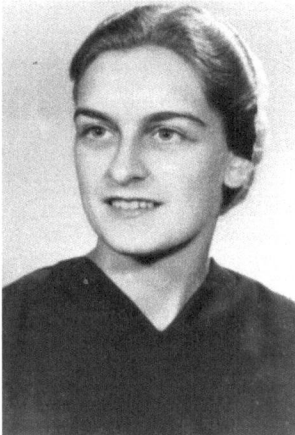

Lancaster Mennonite School students skating on the frozen Millstream that flows through the school campus. Undated newspaper clipping.

rear end stuck up. She got caught. Or we'd hide in closets. One time I was in the closet, and the matron found me. Just things like that.

When the Mill Stream would freeze over in the winter, school was dismissed for the afternoon and we would have a fun time skating.

I took shorthand and typing and accounting in my junior and senior years. I enjoyed accounting, but not when things didn't come out. Probably algebra was my least liked subject; I just had a time with that class. We would work on an algebra problem all night and not get it. But that's how determined I was. I just kept at it until I got it.

We had a good history teacher. He made things very interesting all through history class. In music, everybody had to lead a song. That was a little scary for me. I didn't like to be up front. But we got through it. I probably would have enjoyed home economics if we had had it then, but we didn't have home economics or anything like that.

I will always be thankful to my parents for the sacrifice they made to send me to LMS.

John: I was in elementary school at East Petersburg Elementary during World War II. One of the things that really impacted me over that time was the air raid drills they had. We as a class would leave the classroom. East Petersburg had eight classes: four on the first floor, four on the second floor. On the first floor you'd walk out and sit under the steel stairways, and sit there until the air raid drill was over.

Hempfield was very much into the war. They had drives for everything: paper drives, milkweed pod drives, tin cans. They did anything to get us to realize there's a war going on, and so, therefore, we need to work as a group to beat the other grade in collecting whatever.

We all dressed pretty much the same: there was no distinction of wealthy people—and we had some. There wasn't many different types of clothing to buy, just

John's 3rd grade class, with teacher Miss Barto. John is in the second row, wearing suspenders.

wasn't. We all carried our lunch to school, and believe it or not, we all ate bologna sandwiches and onion sandwiches. An onion sandwich had a quarter inch thick slice, at least, of onion on well-buttered bread. Some toasted their bread a little bit. It had salt on it, and some people put mayonnaise or some kind of other dressing on it.

We ate a lot of onions because that was supposed to be healthy. I often wondered what the classroom smelled like! It almost seemed like the mothers all went together and had the same onion day.

I can name every teacher right up through my school years. Many of them left an imprint on me.

Miss Garrison, my first grade teacher, was single and right out of college. To me she was a gorgeous young lady. She was strict; she was a good teacher. For reading, she had her class divided up into bird sections: cardinals, robins, blue birds, maybe there was one that was a black bird.

I had a back-to-back German measles/mumps affliction in first grade, and it caused me not to be reading. So when I returned to school, she put me back from the cardinals—who were the first birds, number ones—to the number twos, which was a robin. I didn't like that. She said, "Well, you can work your way up." And I did. That was a good lesson for me.

My third grade teacher, Miss Bard, was a Church of the Brethren lady. She was probably in her 50s, and she was a sweetheart of a teacher. All the students loved her. She had a way of dealing with situations that you came out feeling okay.

Fourth grade I had Miss Hershey, and she was 86 years old. She would tell stories—this is, I think, what got me into liking stories and telling stories. She lived

John enjoyed sports and found he had talent. Here shooting basketball at home in a classic Purina Feed cap.

at Wrightsville during the Civil War. She watched with her family the Columbia bridge being burned so that the Confederates wouldn't go across to Lancaster County. Although they did. She had seen Jeb Stuart, the Confederate cavalry leader go over to Lancaster and come back over with a whole bunch of beef cattle. Drive them across the bridge and head south then after they got across. It was good eating for those Southern boys. I enjoyed Miss Hershey.

You get taught how you're supposed to be as a Christian, or how you're supposed to be as a person that loves Jesus. Then you have somebody in your midst who's at the bottom of the poverty level. There was a family that was very poor. These children didn't have much, and sometimes they got picked on. They came in my third grade. It sorted something out for me, in my mind, when I was in fourth grade where I drove a stake and said "I'm going to stick up for people like that. I'm going to help people like that."

So I did. My heart always went out to somebody that struggled, whether it was in a class or for social activities. We had spelling bees and all kinds of challenges: two teams, pick ups. Often times I was one of the leaders of those, and if I would pick somebody that the others didn't think was good, they'd let me know it. But I liked to help those people to feel good about themselves. That has stuck with me. I think that has helped me in making a lot of decisions in life in relation to people.

Fifth grade was a bad grade. Our teacher, soon after school started, got sick. We had five different teachers in fifth grade. That's when more or less I said to myself I don't want to be a school teacher, because we kind of got out of hand as a bunch of students.

For eighth grade I went over to Landisville. Hempfield then became a joint school of all their different grade schools, so we were meeting in what is now the

John's family of origin, 1944, from left: Miriam, Mark, Elam holding James, Elizabeth, Ruth, and John.

administration building. We thought that was a big school. When you look at it now, it looks kind of small.

I enjoyed all my teachers. We had a lot of men—and a couple ladies—that had come out of the military after WWII. There was not much tomfoolery or carrying on because these people ran their classes like we were soldiers in training. You went in properly, and you sat down in order. You followed instructions exactly right, because if you didn't, there was discipline. I mean tough discipline. That's the way it was.

I took a real interest in sports in eighth grade and other extracurricular activities like men's chorale and some plays. Pop didn't like that. I liked all the sports Hempfield had at that point: soccer, basketball, baseball. I don't want to brag or anything, but I think I was pretty good at them. I have gone to some of the dinners that my classmates from Hempfield have, and they remind me of that sometimes. They said, "We wish you would have been able to play for us. We needed you."

I liked drama. I liked music. I wanted to play piano. My sisters could take piano lessons, but not the boys. Just recently when us siblings were together, I asked my sister, Miriam, whether she would have taught me if I would have asked her to. She said, "Never entered my head." Older sister teaching brother that the parents didn't want playing? I think Mom would have stuck up for me.

Pop told me I could not be a part of some of the plays because he thought they would be too "worldly." I did not have to drop out of the mixed choir or the male choir. I could sing along with all that, but Pop and Mom never went to any of those programs. They stayed clear of it; they wanted to be separated from the world.

Pop left me go one more year at Hempfield, ninth grade, then he said I had to go to Lancaster Mennonite. I was angry. I argued with Pop. He said, "There's no use in arguing with me because you are going to go to LMH. I'm sending your records down there. You have to show up." Mark was down at LMH, and so I didn't have a chance. He liked LMH.

I went to LMH my sophomore year. The sports they offered were intramurals.

We had a good basketball team. We went to Virginia and played a team from Eastern Mennonite School during their Holy Week, Holy City. They would sing the "Holy City" chorale, and we went down and played EMS.

A teacher, Miss Catherine Mummaw, set it up, and she took all the flak. We got found out of course. LMH was going to discipline us severely by kicking us out for a while. But she went to bat for us, bless her heart! She took all the blame. Got reprimanded. That was her last year teaching there. I pitied her.

LMH is where I graduated from then. My education was a good education, good teachers basically.

John playing baseball at LMS playing field behind the greenhouses, circa 1954.

Our Journeys Join

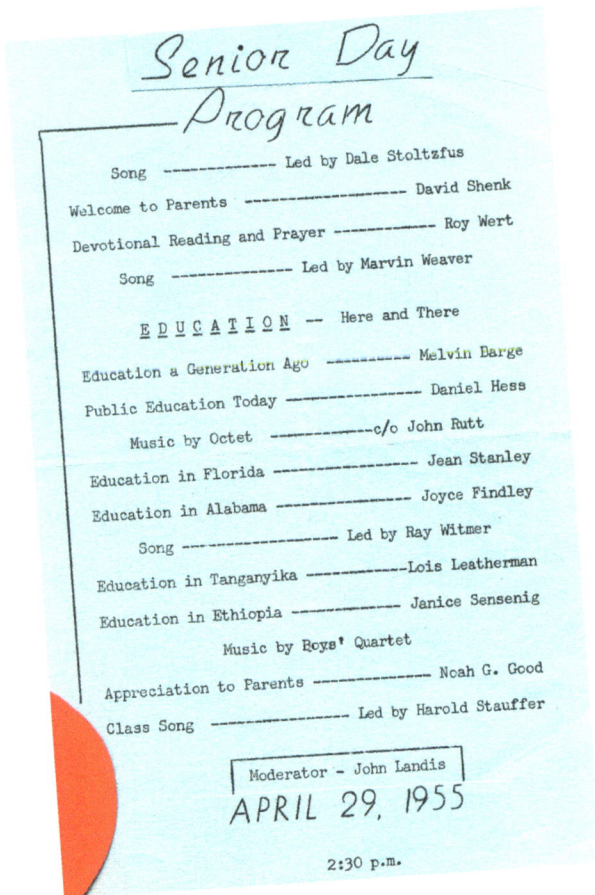

Senior Day Program

```
Senior Day
   Program

Song ------------- Led by Dale Stoltzfus
Welcome to Parents ---------------- David Shenk
Devotional Reading and Prayer ------------ Roy Wert
Song ------------- Led by Marvin Weaver

    E D U C A T I O N -- Here and There

Education a Generation Ago --------- Melvin Barge
Public Education Today --------------- Daniel Hess
   Music by Octet -----------c/o John Rutt
Education in Florida ---------------- Jean Stanley
Education in Alabama --------------- Joyce Findley
      Song ---------------- Led by Ray Witmer
Education in Tanganyika -------------Lois Leatherman
Education in Ethiopia ------------- Janice Sensenig
      Music by Boys' Quartet
Appreciation to Parents ------------- Noah G. Good
Class Song ---------------- Led by Harold Stauffer

      Moderator - John Landis
   APRIL 29, 1955

         2:30 p.m.
```

Eileen and John met at Lancaster Mennonite School, where they were in the same graduating class.

Eileen: *John can make a longer story about how we met and got together than I can! I did date three fellows before him. Two of them were from high school, and one was a local boy here in Lebanon County. John had his eye on me, so he says, and after I finished dating the last one, who I had dated for about three months, John decided he was going to ask me.*

He saw me in the school hallway and came down to where I was going. I went into the bathroom. He waited outside the bathroom door, because he figured I had to come out sometime! That's where he asked me, down at LMH. It was a Thursday or Friday in May. Then Saturday we had our first date to hear B. Charlie Hostetter, who was holding a special meeting at McCaskey High School. That was right before we graduated from high school.

John: Growing up, when Grandpa and Grandma Landis would come to visit us, and before they'd leave, Grandpa would always hunt up Mark and me, and the last part of his conversation was, "Boys, get yourself a good woman for your wife." Always. Mark and I still laugh about that. We used to joke about it then. We weren't even old enough to date!

When I was 15 or 16, I made a list of the qualities that I wanted in my wife. I still have that paper. They were just simple things, good things. That really made me look over women closely, deeper than looks.

I grew up with two neighbor girls who were a bit older than me, Annie Toews and Shirley Brubaker. We planted tobacco together, we worked together, did things. Shirley Brubaker we did most with. I was out there different times to help Pop Brubaker, as we called him, to do things. Shirley was four years older than me.

These were two young ladies that were par excellence. They had excellent manners; they had excellent ways of talking. They didn't sit around and make their mother and father do things; they were up front and doing things for them. They were unusual ladies.

Course I knew I would never date them. When I made this list, I had these two women in the back of my mind. That really kept me from dating a lot of women. There were a lot of girls that are smart, good girls, nothing wrong with them. But there was always something about my list that didn't quite come together with them.

So I didn't date much. At LMH I dated one girl one time, and I felt like she used me. She wanted to go to a party, so I felt like I was used. I dated another girl for three months. She was a wonderful young

John was vice president of the class of '55.

lady. But somehow or other she was not where I was, because we were dating for three months and she thought she had me and somehow or other left that slip. That didn't quite fit my pattern again.

But I was watching Eileen, because I had noticed something unusual about her. I told myself if I get a chance, I'm going to date her. But she dated two fellows for a good part of the senior year.

The one fellow was one of my friends. He said, "John, I'm going to quit Eileen on Sunday night so if you want her you can have her Monday." I said, "Thanks for telling me. How many others did you tell?" He said, "Nobody. You're the only one that knows it; keep it to yourself."

On Monday morning, I saw her walking. She went to three classes, and I could not get to her. But everybody knew that Eileen and Paul weren't dating anymore. She went into the ladies restroom, and I told myself, "You got to pay a price for this." So I stayed outside the girls restroom. When she came out, I walked with her to the next class. In the meantime, I asked her for a date Saturday night. She accepted, which surprised me. Cause if a girl quit a guy or a guy quit a girl, they generally didn't have a date the next weekend. But she accepted.

Eileen: *I'm not sure if there was a quartet there at the time who was singing—it was a special meeting. I suppose they just asked to have it at McCaskey because the auditorium is bigger. At that time we didn't have any public meetings at LMH, although they had an auditorium but it wasn't as nice as McCaskey had. I'm not sure if it was a youth meeting. If I remember right, there were a lot of youth there. They had Youth for Christ meetings; maybe it was a Youth for Christ meeting. I just don't remember.*

In those days when you returned to the house with your date after being out, he only got to the living room. Very seldom did you go to the kitchen together on a date. When I went to get some treat I left John sit in the living room, and I went out and got the treat ready and brought it back in to him. Same way if we double dated. The girls went out to the kitchen and got the treat ready for them; it was much more formal than now. It was just that way. After we were engaged, after we dated quite a while, that was different. You showed him the rest of the house. They were allowed in the kitchen and so forth.

John and I did a lot of double dating with other couples. There were two other couples: his brother, Mark, and wife now, Alma, and then another couple that we did a lot of triple dating, I guess you would call it. We took trips up to northern Pennsylvania and spent the day and things like that.

John: We dated almost three years, I guess. I'll have to tell you that story, too. My dad had this idea that the oldest son needs to marry before the younger son gets married. Bless his heart—where he got it, I don't know.

"Well, there's some problems in that," I told Pop one night. He said, "Why?" I said, "Cause Mark doesn't even have a girlfriend." "That's my way of thinking," he said. "You're going to have to get after Mark."

Mark and I slept together in the same bedroom. I started to work him over.

Mark had dated Alma, and then she quit him because she wasn't sure that this was the one for her. But after she quit Mark, she recanted. She was one of Eileen's good friends, and she told Eileen, "I don't know why I quit Mark. I wish I hadn't." Eileen told me that, so I got after Mark.

He was dating another girl from Manheim, dating her pretty heavy. I said, "Buddy, if you don't have intentions of marrying Liz, you get back to Alma. She'll take you." He hauled around, but lo and behold, he did quit Liz. He said, "Are you sure that Alma will accept me?" I said, "She's ready for you, buddy." I really fed him a line. So he did; he asked her for a date. She accepted.

"Now," I said, "I got a problem, Mark." Cause people knew by now that Eileen and I were engaged. I said, "Pop says I can't marry her until you get married." He just looked at me. He said, "You what?!" I said, "Either you're going to persuade Pop that it's going to be okay for me to get married, or you're going to get married sooner than you're counting on getting married." I pushed him, I really pushed him: "Did you ask her yet? Why don't you ask her?" Same old story, he was afraid that she wouldn't accept him. I said, "How do you know if you don't try it?"

In 1956 Eileen had gone south to teach Bible school. Alma was along with that group of girls. Of course I was writing to Eileen. I guess that made Alma more anxious because here's Eileen getting all these letters. I wrote three letters a week! I can hardly believe it. What did I have to say at that time?

When she came home we went up to the Cornwall fire tower, off of Route 322. We went hiking, just Eileen and I. I had my heart pretty well set that I was going to marry her.

That night there was a beautiful, gorgeous sunset in the west. I'll never forget it; I can picture it in my mind now. We were sitting there in silence for periods of time, talking about the grandeur of the sunset. She was telling about some of the sunsets down south. One thing led to another, and I popped the question. She said yes.

I think she told her sister, Virginia, and she told Alma. To my memory, we didn't tell anybody for a while other than that, but it gave me leverage to push Mark!

It didn't take Mark too long, after Alma came back from the Bible school trip, that he got up the courage and asked her to marry him. They decided to get married in January of '57. Course I was smart-aleck enough to ask him, "Couldn't you get married sooner than that?!"

I said something to my dad after Mark told him that they wanted to get married in January. My Pop could push things to the limit, too. I said something to him about us getting married in '57 yet. He said, "When's your birthday?" I said, "It'll be March of next year." He said, "You know if you wait till then, you can sign your own marriage license?" I said, "Well isn't it an honor if you sign my license?" Mom gave him a dirty look, which I saw. So Pop said, "Ok. If you get married in December, it'll be okay. I'll sign it."

So that created the question of where are we going to live? What're we going to do for a living? I wasn't certain at that point of whether I had to do my 1-W alternative to military service or not, so I was kind of in flux. Mark didn't have to go into 1-W service because he took over his father-in-law's farm and dairy. Farmers could get out of doing alternative service to the military.

I knew, of course, that as soon as I would get married and start farming, I would also be exempt. That's why I wanted to get married sooner, so I could start farming sooner. Our family farmed a couple farms there around Roots Auction near East Petersburg. I was hoping that I would be farming one of those farms.

But instead, in 1956, Pop just gave me an allotted amount of ground, which I think was probably ten acres. I put potatoes out and some tobacco out. 1957 was very dry. The potato crop didn't do well, and neither did the tobacco. That wasn't giving me much money, and I began looking for other farms to rent.

Eileen: *We got married on December 28, 1957. The first two months or so his parents wanted him to do some work at home yet. His mother didn't invite me to come and be there, so we lived separately—I at my home. I didn't like that too much.*

He was helping his dad. They had tobacco, and he had to help strip tobacco. He came to see me Wednesday nights. So that was a surprise, that we couldn't be together those couple months, because that wasn't talked about before we got married.

Eileen and John married December 28, 1957 at Krall's Mennonite Church. With their wedding party, left to right: Daniel Hess, Donald Hershey, Mark Landis, John Landis, Eileen Hart Landis, Virginia Hart, Geraldine Snavely, Arlene Beam.

Cutting the cake, with Mark Landis and Virginia Hart nearby.

John: Pop wanted me to farm the home farm. There was a couple things that forced me to wrestle with my own soul quite a bit because, number one, I would have to grow tobacco. Even though in '57 I had three acres of tobacco, I still wasn't happy about being a tobacco farmer.

Secondly, I knew Pop and Mom were going to move out of the home farm and move into the Brubaker place. We had the Toews' farm, and we had the Kauffman farm. Pop wanted to keep the three smaller farms, which would have given him about 70-some acres, I guess, between the three.

On the issue of growing tobacco, Pop would not give in. I became as stubborn as him. I said, "Pop, I'm not going to grow tobacco." He said, "Well you won't make it if you don't grow tobacco." I said, "I think we can." I knew how to carpenter too. I had done some of that as a single fellow. I said, "Ben Nissley will take me as a carpenter." But he wasn't too happy about that because somebody else would be com-

Eileen preparing a meal on their three-week wedding trip to Florida. Here in St. Augustine, Florida in an exceptionally cool December that damaged the orange crop that year.

A ledger of wedding trip expenses. During the trip, gas was $.15 per gallon and a night at a motel cost about $5.00

ing in there where he felt he should be. Ben Nissley was a reformed Mennonite deacon, very conservative but a very big-hearted man and a good carpenter.

Pop said, "Maybe you better buy equipment awhile." I had some money saved up. He found—why he did that I don't know—he found two tractors, a Farmall and a C Farmall, and he thought I should buy them. So I did, but I still didn't have any place to rent.

Then Eileen's Uncle Clair told me, "I think I know where there's a farm going to be for rent south of Annville." That didn't sit too well with Pop that Eileen's relatives were now getting involved. Later in life when I got into counseling, I could understand, because of my own upbringing, why family systems are so important to understand!

Eileen and I went to the owner of the farm south of Annville and rented it. I went home and told Pop what I did, and he was not a happy camper. I didn't know until years later—he told James, my younger brother—James farmed the home place then years

Invoice showing the first equipment John bought to establish himself in farming, a Farmall M tractor and a Farmall C tractor.

The first farm John rented. It was a 70 acre farm south of Annville, which he rented from Irvin Krall for the 1958-1959 season. John milked 21 cows and farmed 5 acres of potatoes there.

later, 10–12 years later—he said, "You probably never knew this, but Pop wanted you to have the home farm." I said, "Oh? He never told me that." "Well," he said, "I know he didn't. He told me he didn't tell you that, and I told him that it was a mistake: he wanted you to have it but wanted to tell you how to farm."

I told James there's another reason that I didn't know if I wanted to take the home farm. At that time Binkley and Ober Stone Quarry was expanding. The quarry at started on the Haverstick farm. The building sat along Route 72 where the cinder block plant is now. They had bought the Workman farm, which is the first farm out of East Petersburg there next to the Haverstick farm. The Hess farm was right across the street from it. Then they bought the Siegrist farm, which was the next farm out the road.

That meant they were boxing in Pop. I didn't know that at that time, because they still hadn't bought the Workman farm or the Siegrist farm, but I was astute enough to know that this could happen because Pop could not buy the Siegrist farm. He wanted to, but he and old man Siegrist didn't like each other. So that closed the door for Pop to buy that. Pop had made the statement "Some day the quarry's going to buy the Siegrist farm. That'll be the end for this farm."

So I knew all that, and that was another reason. I knew it was going to be valuable property—there was going to be a lot of money involved in it. I knew I had strong sisters, and that my brothers weren't too far on behind. That if I bought that farm and I ended up with a million dollars, I wasn't going to be too well-liked. That was my take. I told James that. He looked at me, he says, "You were smart. What you just said is the truth." I said, "Well, I have observed what other families went through. One person sold the home farm and made a bunch of money and the rest didn't get any. That doesn't go down too well."

So I became a Lebanon county farmer. We farmed one year on Spruce Street in Annville. Then the same man that I was farming for—he had six farms, a little Dutchman, Irvin Krall, he had one down in Schaefferstown he wanted me to farm. He said, "I'll give you first chance at it." So we moved down to Schaefferstown, farmed there seven years. Then he sold it away from me.

I thought I had it bought. I learned you got to seal it immediately if you want to buy land. I had bought it for $60,000, a good neighbor arrangement, verbal. We were busy in the fields, and we had kind of agreed that we'd go to a lawyer as soon as we had some free time.

John farming.

I saw this man out walking around the barn and looking things over. Told Eileen I got to go see what that man's doing. I went out, and he told me he was looking it over because he wanted to see what he had bought. I said, "May I ask what you paid for it?" He told me. So I wished him the best. Then I told Eileen, and she was upset.

It was one of those years that there was just nothing available. Tried to buy a farm, then Irvie said to me, "By Annville's a farm as big as this farm, and I'll put a new dairy barn in, silo, milkhouse. You want to move up there? I'll give you first chance at it." I was going to pay rent so much an acre then. So we took it. We spent 13 years living there.

I tried to buy the farm off of Irvie. He wouldn't sell it to me because he said he had promised it to his granddaughter. Well, I knew what his grandchildren were like. Irvie had spoiled his two grandchildren. He had a grandson and a granddaughter. I managed to rent more land. I was farming close to 400 acres and had 60 cows.

You never know what you might get in for! Here Keith (blue jacket) and Darryl (yellow shirt) holding the step ladder on top of the Allis-Chalmers 200 tractor so that John can rescue a small gas-powered model airplane that got tangled in a telephone line at the Ebersole farm, circa 1978.

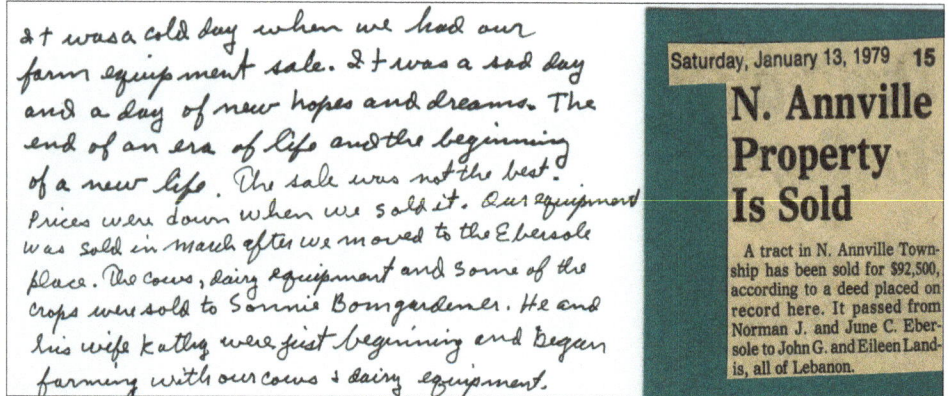

It was a cold day when we had our farm equipment sale. It was a sad day and a day of new hopes and dreams. The end of an era of life and the beginning of a new life. The sale was not the best. Prices were down when we sold it. Our equipment was sold in March after we moved to the Ebersole place. The cows, dairy equipment and some of the crops were sold to Sonnie Bomgardener. He and his wife Kathy were just beginning and began farming with our cows & dairy equipment.

Saturday, January 13, 1979 15

N. Annville Property Is Sold

A tract in N. Annville Township has been sold for $92,500, according to a deed placed on record here. It passed from Norman J. and June C. Ebersole to John G. and Eileen Landis, all of Lebanon.

Irvie died. It was 1977 and this man came in one day and said to me, "Here I got a piece of paper I want you to sign." It said I have to pay rent of $100 an acre. I said, "When would this start?" He said, "Well, it says there immediately."

I said, "I don't know who you are. I don't know what kind of man you are. But apparently, you're not too honest." I told him that right to his face, which he didn't like. He was some insurance dealer, then I found out. I said, "You're coming to me with a piece of paper that says my landlord wants me to either leave this place in three months or pay $100 an acre rent for it? Are you aware that I farm about 300 acres more than what this farm is? And I pay $50 an acre. The land is just as good. That's the going price right now of land to rent around here."

He said, "You'll pay $100 an acre starting on October 1 or I'll have you thrown out." He was as ticked at me as I was at him. I just looked at him. Mennonite or not Mennonite, pastor or not pastor—which I was at that time—I said, "If I'd be you, I wouldn't try that." He said, "Why not?" I said, "I'll nail your wings to the wall. I got a lawyer. You're not going to do that to me." He said, "Then you better be out."

I said, "Can you see the driveway?" "Yeah," he said, "What about it?" I said, "I want to see your car leaving this driveway now." I was ticked. I was cheated. It was corrupt, and I told the guy that.

I sold my cows and my dairy equipment to a young couple that wanted to leave his father—he was working for his father. I sold the hay, silage, all that stuff. We had two assessors come in—he picked one, I picked another one—and they agreed on the price of all this stuff. So we settled on that. I had quite a bit of big equipment that I could sell at a public sale, which I did then, because I didn't have any place to store it. My other properties didn't have buildings, so I was caught there.

That taught me an awful lot about dealings with people. I learned it doesn't matter who the person is that you're working with, be careful. You may not be able to trust them. These were good church people. Money talks, doesn't matter who it is, money talks.

Ex-Dairy Farmer Now Raises Ber

John Landis of North Annville Township was a dairy farmer for 21 years when he decided to make a change in his occupation. The rent was getting too high on the farm and he was unable to buy it. So he decided to trade in the cows for strawberry and other plants.

Today, he and his wife, Eileen, have 22 acres on which they commercially grow strawberries, black and red raspberries, asparagus, cauliflour and sugar peas. The berries and peas are Pick-Your-Own.

Landis says he doesn't miss the twice-a-day, all-year-round milkings, but he does miss the regular milkchecks. His work on the crops is only seasonal, but he still has the risks from depending so heavily on Mother Nature. And, as with dairy farming, he must still keep a watchful eye on costs and still worries about prices.

In addition, whereas dairy farmers as a collective force see their competition from afar—chiefly the soft drink people—Landis knows his competition to be other strawberry growers. There are 24 in the county compared to four or five eight years ago. Consequently, there is overproduction.

Eight of his acres are in strawberries. Thursday marked the first day for picking and word of mouth about this fact, before his advertising started Friday, had already brought a small number of pickers by mid-afternoon that day. A foursome, armed with empty boxes, walks out to the fields. Landis recognizes them as past customers.

"You know how to pick. These berries have a lot of white tips. Please leave them here," he says referring to the berries not ripe yet.

The pride of his strawberries is his Early Glow, a type that he says is sweeter than his Rariton or Lester, and that keeps well. He points to one patch that was planted six years ago and, amazingly, is producing well this season. That is unexpected because strawberry plants choke themselves off eventually and should be replaced every three to four years for better production and health. Nonetheless, some home gardeners keep their plants for up to 12 years.

Talking like he knows his crops, he says strawberries need water and sunlight and need fertilization and to be weedfree. Humidity, cloudy weather and too much rain are not good for them. They bring fungus, rot and insects.

To get rid of weeds he has to work by hand, as the herbicide Roundup not only kills the weeds but the plants, too, he explains. Sometimes the thistles get so thick he has to apply Roundup anyway, as he did last year, reluctantly wiping out a corner of the strawberries in the process.

Watering is by sprinkler irrigation, through long pipes running between the rows.

The raspberries are not ready for harvest until about July 4, Landis says. The reds, which are too popular in this area, are Latham and Heritage and the blacks Cumberland and Bristol. The black

Dave
Knauss

Around
The
Farm

grows hybrids Jersey Giant and Mary Washington. It is a big seller, leading him to plant a new patch this spring.

Asparagus is not hard to grow, Landis says. It likes a lot of fertilizer. After planting, one is wise to wait until the third year before picking to allow the root system to develop. Then the spears start coming up, and it pays to know how to cut the spears. Commercial growers cut them off at three or four inches under the ground to increase weight but the bottoms are tough. Amateur pickers may break them off too high, wasting much of them. Landis breaks them off just above the ground.

Asparagus growth is highly dependent on the weather, Landis says. Incredibly, the spears can grow several inches in a day if it is warm and sunny, like Thursday was.

The cauliflour is planted in late summer for fall harvest and Landis picks that and sells wholesale.

There are times, like with a bad crop, that Landis wishes he never would have gotten into berry and vegetable growing. But there are many other times he enjoys the same experiences that all other farmers do. Such as when he comes out very early in the morning to pick asparagus. The sun is just coming up; a light dew rests on the grass and crops; it is pleasantly cool, and a killdeer bird cries out at him every time he walks past the nest at a certain time of year.

He also enjoys the people that

come to his farm. "Generally people that come to pick their own are nice people," he says. "They're easy to get along with, although there are a few you wish wouldn't come back. I enjoy meeting people and seeing the same ones year after year, learning how their families are doing."

The Landises have five of their own children, four of them in college and one graduated. None have stayed on the farm, opting for the professions. To help pay for college tuition and his and his wife's own expenses, Landis has other income: He is pastor at Gingrich's Mennonite Church, does some public speaking, and takes part-time work in the off-season such as being maintenance man at United Christian Church Home near Annville last winter. In the cold months he also has time to go to fruit and vegetable growers'

meetings.

In the spring he has to have his mind back on his crops to ensure a good harvest. Three years ago he lost a crop due to frost. He learned from that. There was frost three times this spring after the berries blossomed but each time Landis turned on the sprinkler and saved them.

The ball field on the Landis farm near Annville served the local community.

I did find a 23 acre place north of Annville. The people that we bought the farm from, this little farm, gave us a good deal. When we moved back here I put in a ball field on the farm. That was another mistake. It cost me $10,000 to grade the ground to put in the ball field and the backstop. I did it on the premise that the churches and the local softball league was going to pay for it. Well, they didn't, even though they used it a lot.

Again, that whole thing of thinking things through to make sure that you really want to do this. How many times do I have to do something that I get caught?

Hart Landis Family Life

Eileen: *We didn't have any children for the first five years of our marriage. I think that was good. We learned to know each other; we had fun. You didn't have to be concerned about a child or anything like that in those five years. We were constantly together. We could be, and we were.*

My dad and John would work together quite a bit in those years too. But that ended May 19, 1961 when my dad died, a very sad day for our family. Dad had built a second-story chicken house between the barn and another shed. He had chickens up there, and the manure became too heavy. He was trying to block it up to reinforce the floor, and it fell on him. It killed him right away.

We were at home when my mother called us to come up. We lived at Schaefferstown, about a half hour away, and we got there in record time. John drove like crazy. My mother couldn't go out to see what was going on because she was in a wheelchair. My sister Virginia was at home with my mother. They heard a noise and looked out the kitchen door and saw chickens and dirt flying everywhere.

We got there, and John got out to check what was going on. He wouldn't let me go along. He said, "You stay in here," which I'm glad he did, because he has a memory that I didn't need to have. My father was 51.

My mother and two sisters and a brother moved in with us after my dad died. We had a house that had five rooms upstairs and five rooms downstairs, so we had plenty of room, but that was an adjustment. I guess as life comes, I learn to flow with whatever comes.

My sister, Virginia, got married during that time, so then it was only three of them staying with us. After my sister got married, my mother said that she thinks now she should make a home for her two younger children, and they moved to Paradise. They had lived with us for about a year or two.

As it turned out, we had our five children in five years. I was a busy mother! Our first child, Darryl, was born in 1962. Keith came not quite two years later, and Rose followed ten months behind Keith. Then we had twins at the end—Dwight and Dwayne. Darryl was about five and a half years old when the twins were born.

John and Eileen, enjoying each other's company, 1960. Location: in the living room of their second farmhouse on Prescott Road, Shaefferstown, PA.

News article featuring Eileen's father, Jacob, and his farming. Features first milking parlor in Lebanon County, which was installed on his dairy farm on Starner Road September 1, 1951. Lebanon Daily News, Thanksgiving Day, 1951.

"My dad and John would work together quite a bit in those years."

"The Only Way to Milk"

"It's the only way to milk cows," is what Jacob Hart, Route 5, Lebanon, Pa., says about parlor milking.

He believes that this easy way of taking care of an otherwise laborsome chore is the most natural way for a cow to be milked. He particularly likes the adaptability of the parlor system to any number of cows without having to add more barn.

His present Surge milking parlor used to be an old implement shed and the conversion didn't take a mint of money. He paid only $432 to have a tile wall built on one side, and this price included all concrete work done on the elevated platform where the cows stand and the milker's alley floor. Then came $180 worth of concrete blocks and his three Surge Parlor Stalls plus his own labor. In all, it was a cheap conversion which is bringing fine results.

Hart milks 13 Holsteins and ships to the Puritan Dairy. From there the product goes to New York City. He's never been bothered with a kicking cow since beginning his parlor milking Sept. 1, 1951. It took only two or three milkings for his cows to become used to their new milking quarters and since then they've behaved like veterans.

THIS PENNSYLVANIA FARMER isa't a big milk producer but he has seen the value in the parlor system of milking cows. His name is Jacob Hart and he milks 13 cows in his three-stall parlor.

It was a challenge. People used to tell me, "These times will go fast," and I thought, oh my, I don't know! I was washing diapers all the time. I often pitied the second one, Keith, with his sister coming along ten months later. When I went to put them in bed, I remember I wasn't supposed to carry or lift heavy, so I would have him crawl up the steps and bring Rose along in my arms. I think at different times that wasn't very nice, but I didn't know what else to do.

Now I think, looking back, even though I had five children in five years, I think I would have tried to spend more time individually with each one. When they were that close, you sort of clumped them all together and did activities that they could all enjoy.

I just tried to keep my head above water. I remember one thing I did for getting them all ready for church. I would bathe them and have them all ready except the outer clothes, because I didn't want them to go to church spotted or dirty. Then we'd put their dresses on and suits on at the last minute. I remember doing that until they would grow old enough to get dressed themselves.

John was very helpful and very understanding, but he was also farming. One time I still had the breakfast dishes on the table when he came in for dinner. I said, "I'm sorry, I just didn't get around to it." He said, "That's ok, your children are more important now." So he was understanding that way. If I didn't get things done like I wanted to, why, he accepted that.

Him being a farmer, he could help. Often, if they got to me or something, I'd tell them to go out to the barn to their dad, and that would give me a break for a while. If he had been working away somewhere, I probably would have minded it much much more.

Neighbors Aid Bereaved Family

Seventeen neighbors turned out Wednesday and Thursday to plant corn for the family of Jacob H. Hart, Lebanon RD 5. Hart was killed last Friday afternoon when a chicken house collapsed on him.

The action is reminiscent of another era: — a gentle, unhurried time when friendship meant something more than just a possible future business or social contact.

The tragedy at the Hart farm, located a half-mile west of Quentin, occurred at the worst possible time for a farm family: spring planting time.

And so, even though the days are severely numbered this time of the year for proper planting and soil consistency, neighbors pushed their persona. planting schedules back a few days to help a family among them in distress.

The question was never "Will you help?", but "When can we help?" So, when Levi Mumma sent word out to meet Wednesday morning bright and early at the Hart cornfield, men and equipment converged from all sides.

(Continued on Page Twenty-one)

GOOD NEIGHBOR POLICY—Neighbors of the late Jacob Hart, Lebanon RD 5, who was killed last Friday in a farm accident, prepare his fields for corn planting. Seventeen neighbors prepared and planted 30 acres in two days.

Daily NEWS Photo

Neighbors Aid Bereaved Family With Planting

(Continued From Page One)

Clair Hart, Annville RD 1, a brother of the deceased, brought his big tractor up and acted as a coordinator for the planting activities. However, he noted that all the volunteers were seasoned farmers and didn't need much coordinating. He said, "We all work together No bosses here."

Took Two Days

Processing 30 acres in two days is no mean feat. First there was fertilizer to be spread, then plowing and discing, then the planting of the corn. Any farmer knows that there are plenty of other steps in between.

Mrs. Elizabeth Hart, the widow, voiced this reaction to the generous action: "I just think it's wonderful that I have such good neighbors and friends. We appreciate everything that has been done for us. I don't know how to say thank you."

Although the bereaved Hart family were Mennonites, most of their neighbors are not.

She expressed special appreciation to John Landis, Myerstown RD 2, her son-in-law. He and his wife, Eileen, have been constant companions to the girl's mother since the tragedy.

Children at ome with Mrs. Hart are Virginia, 20; Dervin, 17, and Carleen, 11.

On Wednesday neighbors spent a large part of the day cleaning the chicken house, using the manure as fertilizer for the corn field. Seventeen men worked both Wednesday and Thursday. They started about 8:30 in the morning and finished up about 5:00 each evening.

Equipment that was in use Wednesday included one loader, six spreaders and seven tractors.

On Thursday six disc harrows and one seed planter were in operation. Four plows and two spreaders worked ahead of the discs and the seeder. A total of 13 tractors were on the scene Thursday at one time or another.

Neighbors helping were: Levi Mumma and son, Robert; Clair Hart, Annville RD 1; Dervin Hart, who was assisted by his brother-in-law, John Brandt, Robert Kreider, Amos Weaver, Mays Kurtz, Mays Kurtz Jr., Harry Kurtz, Lloyd Early; Harold Sauders, Mark Hershey, assisted by three employes, Earl Hershey, Willard Wenger and LeRoy Heagy; Allen Dundore, Leroy Leach, Homer Kreider Jr., Clarence Mase, Marvin Mase, Jesse Wine, Robert Martin and Hector Alvarado, an employe of Harold Frey.

[Handwritten note:] May 19, 1961 was a sad day For our Family. Mother lost her loving husband and we children lost our wonderful Father.

[Handwritten note:] I REMEMBER:
— Daddy as a man who loved the Lord and his Family.
— Helping Daddy with milking, baling hay, discing.

County Farmer Dies As Chicken House Collapses

Jacob H. Hart, 50-year-old farmer of Lebanon RD 5, was crushed to death Friday afternoon when the second floor of a chicken house collapsed on him.

The victim, who was using tools in trying to reinforce the building, was completely buried by lumber and manure, according to neighbors who removed

[Handwritten note:] - Daddy holding me on his lap, telling me Mother was very sick but we will work Together and we did. Daddy reading his Bible early in the morning before going to the barn.

Local newspaper clipping describing how 17 neighbors helped by planting Hart family fields five days after Eileen's father died in a farm accident, May 1961, on their farm on Starner Road. Note Eileen's handwritten memories of her dad.

good supper + John had a good talk on Governing Marriages. Children all went to gym night at EICO and Rosie went to Cindy Musser's overnight.

Saturday   Mar. 8

John went to Minister's Meeting at Jim Idesses. The wives were invited, too but I stayed home this morning as the children wanted to go to Myerstown to go to York for a Sports Competition at 12:30. We cleaned this morn. + were ready to leave at 11:30. Had to keep after the boys to keep working. They were still having their meeting so I stood outside the door & waited until they dismissed for dinner at 12:40. Paul Miller talked this morning on the Spiritual Diet of the Congregation + after dinner talked on Celebration. John studied a little when we got home + then we went along with David + June Idesgy to Emil's Restaurant at Manheim for a Sweet-heart Banquet which David + June gave for their church. I had a

Sunday   Mar. 9

Slept till almost 7:30. Abe had the sermon this morn. and introduced 3 families + titus Martin, Nate Elewsole + Roy Weaver. Dwight went along home with Fudds. Duwayne was provoked because he couldn't go along. After dinner John + I went to visit Dennis + Joanne Stouffer. Had a nice visit with them. We were there until 3:30 + then we went Bob + Jean Weaver by 4:15. Had a good visit with them + had supper with them. The Boys were home all after-noon by themselves. We all went to church this evening for our first eve. of revival with Aaron Hollinger as the Evangelist. A nice group were there. Margaret said Barb is coming to see her tomorrow at 9:00. Praise the Lord she is coming for help. A beautiful day – in the 60's + sunny.

Two ordinary, busy days in Landis family life, as recorded by Eileen in her March 8 and 9, 1980, diary entries.

The fact that he was right there and could help, really helped a lot in those years.

When it came to discipline, sometimes they had to sit; sometimes I separated two. Occasionally we spanked. I didn't do much of that because I felt when I spanked I didn't get through to them. I remember chasing Darryl around the table, and well, I couldn't catch him!

There weren't many books printed fifty years ago on parenting. There was Dr. Spock, but I didn't agree with him on everything.

We tried to show that when we said no, we meant no. We probably expected a lot out of them. When we went to church, we expected them to be quiet, which they usually were. Occasionally they weren't. Elm Street was a church that if you wanted to take your child out, the door went to the out of doors. You didn't have a nanny room or someplace else. I took them out a couple times. I guess I just talked to them and then went back in. That's the way it was.

A friend and I were talking recently and she said, "I remember you saying one time, 'Don't let your children on the floor at church because when they get on the floor, they just move around and so forth.'" I asked, "I said that?" "Yes, you said that!"

At Elm Street we had to sit separate during church: men on one side and women on the other side of the church. We split the five children between us, so I only had two or three to watch and John had two or three. The twins were born in 1968, and we started going to Gingrichs to church in 1969. Gingrichs was a little more progressive, and women and men were sitting together. That was an adjustment!

Another thing I did was I usually tried to have dinner in the oven, or something quick, so that when we came home from church, as soon as they got their clothes changed, dinner was ready. They were hungry, and I figured that way I can keep them from snacking and we can eat and they can be satisfied.

When the children were growing up, I don't think I had other interests because all my energy went to family life.

When they were younger, I went to Scofield Bible class once a week with some neighbor ladies. John thought I needed to get out, which I did. When the children were a little older, the youngest ones about ten, is the first time I got a job outside the home and farm. At 44 years old that was a challenge to go for an interview and so forth.

Later on I heard or saw in the paper that Countryside Christian Community retirement home near Annville was

Elm Street Mennonite Church, Lebanon, Pennsylvania. The church was established in a converted car garage and dedicated on October 23, 1955.

Eileen and John catching a bite to eat on a typical, busy day. Note kitchen renovation underway, at the Ebersole Farm on Thompson Avenue, Lebanon, PA, circa 1978.

Celebration for Eileen at her retirement, in 2002, from the Dietary Supervisor role at Countryside Christian Community.

needing a cook. Well, I loved to cook! I went and they hired me, and I worked part-time 5:30-2:00 three days a week. That way I was home when the children came home. The only disadvantage was I had to work every other weekend. We managed.

After a period of time I was asked to be Dietary Supervisor in the kitchen, and I had to take some courses to do that. I managed about a dozen staff. I did that until I was 65 and trained another girl to take my place.

John: Even today when I think about it, I think, my what poor preparation you had for being a father! I was raised under strict discipline, and I anticipated that our children would be strictly disciplined too. I soon realized that these are little babies, little children, not adults, that I can't talk to them. So I had to really work at changing my approach to children. I loved them dearly. The children were a blessing.

I think Eileen's the one that thought we should have something special for the children every evening before they went to bed. So we always read to our children for years, according to their level of understanding. A book or a story and then had hot chocolate—sometimes cookies—before they went to bed. That became a ritual.

Momma could be there with the children on her lap or around her, and I could be alongside. Sometimes she read the story; sometimes I read the story. Sometimes I acted out the story. They seemed to love it. It put them to bed, and we didn't have trouble getting our children to bed. That was a real blessing. And sweet. I never asked them what for impact that may have left on them, but it impacted me.

When we moved to the one farm before we moved back here, it had a stone fireplace that they had closed up. I asked the landlord if I could open it up and rebuild it, and I did. In the wintertime, it was always a nice cozy place to be and do things together as a family.

I enjoyed being a dad. I still do. A surprise is that you never quit being a parent! All of our children are 50 or older now, and they still seek advice and have a very caring love for us.

When I tell people that our children still come back and talk to us about the events of their lives, talk about personal things, talk about their finances, talk about anything, spiritual growth or whatever, they say, "How do you get them to do that?" I don't make them do it. They just come.

I did counseling—marriage and family counseling as a pastor and as part of Jubilee Ministries—and that amazes me when I hear stories other people have of

John playing with, left to right, Darryl, Rose, and Keith in the farmhouse on Royal Road, about 1966.

their families and of their children. I just thank God that Eileen and I had a different story, a beautiful story that love can be shared with children.

We didn't have children that weren't rambunctious either. They were as nixie as anybody's children, which I guess they got from me, I don't know. They were lively, full of energy. You just have to direct that energy in the right way, that's all.

Consistent, appropriate discipline helped. Eileen had a little stick that she had above the doorway into the living room. If they got too out of hand for her, she'd walk over there and get the little stick and that was it.

They found that Dad would always give them extra work to do if they didn't pony up and do what they needed to do. That was the biggest thing I guess I did, just increase their workload. No child likes that!

Children need their fun times. They need to know that their parents will give them that time to have fun. We'd go into the appliance store and bring home great big boxes and tell them, "Here, build yourself something." They would do that.

We had a neighbor that had a swimming pool. He didn't use it because he didn't like taking care of it. So I made an arrangement that lasted for years, that I would take care of his swimming pool, and we had free swimming. A lot of times I'd say, "We have *this* much work we should get done today, and after that, we'll go swimming." They loved that on warm weather days.

The children were in sports in school and also in the community. We went to as many games as we could. I built a ball field on the farm towards the end of the '60s or beginning of the '70s. Again, it's providing the opportunity for them to play.

Inside the one shed I had a basketball court. I always had a lot of energy, and they had a lot of energy. That was a good way to expend it, to get them to feel like they're part of things, the enjoyment of life. But they knew they had to work, too.

Inclusiveness is something Eileen and I both wanted for our children, for them to feel part of a family unit. That was important for us. So we went camping, we did things together, traveled together.

Eileen: *We took time out for fun. We went on a vacation four or five days every year to a cabin upstate. It wasn't an expensive vacation, but we went. We went to a trip out west for six weeks when the oldest was about fifteen.*

John: We had fun together, learned together, and that was great.

The one thing that was unpleasant, I guess, is that every one of our children was in an accident or something. They each faced death or were taken to the hospital, and we were told that they may not make it.

Sharing lunch on a family camping outing. Left to right: John, Dwayne, Darryl, Keith, Dwight, Rose, about 1977.

The family enjoyed many happy annual vacations to this cabin in Sullivan County. The boys tubing at the cabin, right; Eileen and Darryl making egg salad, below left.

They all made it. Those experiences too helped to build us as a family, helped to put us together in a more solid, more caring unit.

Eileen: *Our children were in the 10 to 15 age bracket when we were approached by Philhaven to take care of people that were not bad enough to be in the hospital yet, but were not well enough to go to their homes. They may have been from out of state and didn't live nearby. And so we did that. I don't know how many years we had adults in our home that needed help.*

We weren't expected to give them counsel, but we did have to see that most of them got to Philhaven either for the day or for appointments or something like that.

We had some interesting people over that time! One girl overdosed on something. She told us that she overdosed, and we called Philhaven or the doctor, I'm not sure which. They said to give her some kind of spice in water to cause her to throw up. She was to drink it. She drank it right down. We said, "That's not working."

"Give her soapy water then." Well, she drank that and drank and drank and drank. We told them that it didn't work, she doesn't bring anything up. So they said to take her to the hospital.

Enjoying a six week vacation through the western U.S. Left to right: Keith, Eileen, Dwight, Dwayne (seated), Darryl, Rose.

John and I took her to the hospital. John went along in with her. I don't know if I sat in the waiting room or what. He said she just threw up and threw up and threw up more water. She had water everywhere. They told us to take her to Philhaven. On the way there I sat in the back seat with her, and John drove. She tried to crawl out of the car a couple times. She was a determined to kill herself.

We got her up to Philhaven, and the fellow on duty that night said, "We can't take her." John said, "Well, I'm not taking her back home; you have to take her." The worker didn't think she was as bad as she was. John, the girl, and this worker walked around the hospital a couple times. She tried to bolt out on the road. Then they believed us and admitted her.

She was from New York somewhere. We had contact with her for quite a while afterwards, but we don't anymore.

The people Philhaven asked us to host usually stayed with us anywhere from a couple weeks to a couple months. When my daughter, Rose, was five or six years old, a woman named Lois stayed with us for a time. I would tell Rose to wash dishes or something, and Lois would say she'd do it. Well, Rose soon caught on to this: whatever I told her to do, she'd let Lois do!

I tried to tell Lois different times, she must let Rose do what she's supposed to do. Lois would volunteer to do Rose's work, and then Lois would do it. I just couldn't have that. So we asked her to leave.

John: When we went to Elm Street to church, we walked and visited every home in a three-block area around the church. We talked to them. Most people had a lot of problems.

Next to the church, across from the dike, was a family that was poor. The church went in to help them. The social worker was there. The woman had a baby boy, it was probably one and a half months old, and there were sores all over it. She didn't know anything about mothering: she threw all the dirty diapers down the basement steps. We cleaned that out. The social worker told Eileen to take the baby home, to take care of him. So we took him home.

We got a call two days later from the state police that they're coming out to get that baby, and they might arrest us for kidnapping.

I had a good talk with the trooper. He saw the baby then, too. He said, "Well, the law's the law. I'm not going to arrest you, but make sure you clear everything with papers that are signed. That social worker didn't do her work right." The social worker was as much to blame as we were. Well, that taught me a big lesson. You learn by experience.

Eileen: *Jim Peshina—we called him our foster child for lack of a better word—was not given to us under the system. He was 18 when he came to us, and we learned to know him* *through his sister. There was a group of friends at church who were house parents for a group of girls that were having problems, not necessarily mental problems but just problems with drugs and so forth. He used to come and visit his sister at this home. He had a troubled background. Anyway, he stayed at our house when he was visiting her.*

Jim was in the foster care system, and when he was 18 they were ready to dismiss him from the system. They gave him something like $300, and he was supposed to make it on his own! They asked him if he had any place he'd like to go. He said, "John Landis." They called us and wondered if we would take him.

John and I talked about it, and we decided, "Well, he'll have to go to church with us, and he daren't do drugs or smoke." I think those were the three things. We called the counselor back and told him that he has to go to church, can't drink, can't smoke. The counselor said, "Well, he's crazy." But anyway, Jim came to live with us.

We went through a lot with him. He was a little bit older than our oldest, but emotionally he was like a ten year old, eleven year old. He didn't have much direction in his life, so the issue that he was a little older than our son wasn't really an issue at all because of his upbringing.

As a last ditch effort, we had sent him to many programs like Teen Challenge and homes like that. He'd walk off or he wouldn't stay there. Finally, it got to the place where we told him that he has to either pony up or leave, because it was just too much. He decided to stay and decided he'd go to Rosedale Bible College in Ohio.

He got married to a girl from Rosedale, ran a successful cleaning business, and did well. Jim taught me a lot; he taught the family a lot. I think that's one reason why our children are in jobs that help people—one's a doctor, two of them are nurses—it made them more aware of the hurts that people have.

I Believe

Written by John G. Landis in 1977

God is everything He says
God can do everything He says He can
Jesus is the one and only Son of God
I am everything God says I am
I can do everything through Jesus
Purpose for living is Jesus and his will
I am saved to serve my Lord Jesus Christ
Submission to Jesus is the way of peace
I can only know Jesus as I obey Him
The Bible is the only God breathed "Word"
Jesus is the Alpha and Omega—He is, was,
   and will continue to be

John: We had people out with us, helping us, living with us. I trust people. There are some people you can't trust, I'm aware of that. I'm sure there may have been some things stolen from us.

We were coming down from Pine Grove one time on Route 81, and it was cold, windy. I saw this car with blinkers on ahead. Then I saw somebody get out and start waving a blanket right before I got there. Eileen said, "You can't stop. They're going to rob us." I said, "No." So I stopped, backed up, and got out.

A woman said, "We ran out of gas. We're from New York City, and we're going to Harrisburg. Can you help us?" I looked her over and said, "Do you have a baby in the car?" "Yes." Cause she had a baby blanket, that's what she waved. I said, "Who else is with you?" "My mother and a sister." So I said, "You all come over and get in my car. I have a station wagon. We'll go and get some gas and bring it back and get your car started, and you can go to Harrisburg."

They got in the car. We had a good talk on the way to the gas station. I had to buy a gas can. The guy at the gas station wouldn't trust me with his gas can. Took it back, filled it up. I said, "Pump your throttle a little bit, about three, four times. Then try to start it." It went off, started. I said, "You were along when we got this gas. I want you to come back to that gas station, and I'll fill your car up with gas."

When I was filling her car up with gas, she said, "Who are you? Who are you?" "I'm John, just a follower of Jesus. You know him?" "Well, we go to church sometimes." I said, "Well, do they talk about Jesus?" I knew the gas tank was going to soon be filled. She said, "I don't know much about him." I said, "You ask your pastor, someone there at your church to explain Jesus to you. That's why I do it." I just feel that the Lord wants us to be, everything we study he wants us to be.

There was a lady down in Schaefferstown, filching off of church people. She came in to us where we lived on a dairy farm. She was doing the same thing of begging and selling. I loaded her up: we gave her potatoes, we gave her vegetables from the garden, we gave her milk, eggs. She started to beg to not take anymore.

When it came time for her to go, I stood in front of her door. I said, "Now you haven't asked at all why I'm doing this. Do you want to know?" She said, "Yeah." So I told her. Preached her a little sermon, really. She said, "Thank you." She got in the car, took off. You know, that ended all her going around the community and getting free items. I don't know what she did, whether she left the area or what, but I leave that up to the Lord. I did what I could do, and let the Lord take over from there. That's the way I did things.

I'd see guys in town because I walked the streets pretty often, I'd get to see guys that I knew were hungry. They didn't have any money. I'd say, "Are you guys hungry?" "Yeah." We had a couple restaurants there in Lebanon, so I'd take them in, tell the head guy, "Feed these guys. Here's 20 bucks or 30 bucks to see that they get plenty of food and the tip for you." And I'd leave.

We're supposed to help people, do things for people. How many people do that? I don't know, I don't care if they do it or don't do it. I would like them to do it.

To Minister and Lead

I had a call to serve the church when I was probably 15 or 16. After that, I did a lot of things in the church. I only felt the call to pastoring in my late 50s. Before that, I was very active in doing things in the church, developing things, giving leadership to things, was used by the conference, and I wasn't a minister. I was an ordinary person full of ideas.

Somewhere around 1970 I felt a definite call because we didn't have a pastor at Gingrichs. Eileen and I had left Elm Street, which became a Conservative Conference church in 1968. We left there and went to Gingrichs because we only lived a half mile from the church. It was close for us, and so we went there.

At Gingrichs I became the Sunday school teacher of the young marrieds class. They had quite a few individuals there at Gingrichs at that time who were young people that were of marriageable age, and they were getting married. So I was given that class, and it grew. Seemed like when young couples from other churches would get married, they would come to Gingrichs. Some of that reason was because of me and my teaching.

Gingrichs Mennonite Church, Lebanon, PA.

Come Ye   Mt. 11:28-30

I. Intro:
  - One of the sweetest words is come!

II. An Invitation to Come:
  A. A Choice = v. 1-14 = John Baptist or Pharisees
    1. Who did you go into the desert to see?
    2. He is Elijah, if you accept it?

  B. A Comparison = v. 16-24
    1. Spoiled children = we played/danced + you don't join us
    2. John & Jesus don't fit into your mold either
    3. The ungodly of the past would repent if
      - Chorazin   (Tyre)
      - Bethsaida   (Sidon)
      - Capernaum = Sodom
      - they would have experienced what you are
      - Rejection of Jesus brings judgment
        - not accepting & following as a disciple

  C. A Call = v. 28
    1. Come to me
      - Fathers Pleasure = v. 26
      - Fathers Revelation = v. 27   Jn. 4
      - Father & Son's choice = v. 27   - Samaritan woman

III. Come Ye for the
     - Provisions offered   - no consumerism here
                                 - Jesus is a giver
  A. Rest, Relief = From religious system of that day
    - so much to do 1. From fatigue + weariness + burdens
    - So many good   - trying to work out own salvation
      things to be involved with - loaded down with theologies, philosophies others put on you
    - So little time to rest 2. From vain, fruitless striving after
                              - Peace, Contentment, hope, love, joy
    3. From suffering, unrest, guilty conscience which
       add to the burden + toiling

  B. An easy yoke - bond
    1. connection of life
    2.   "   " Power   - not just a cordless tool but
    3.   "   " Faith   a direct hook up.
    4.   "   " hope
    5.   "   " grace

  C. A light burden
    1. obligation   Mephibosheth
      - to walk with Jesus, the king   II Sam. 9
      - to serve with Jesus, the king
      - to love
    2. identification   (Peter at trial of Jesus by maid.
      - Be with   "You were with him!")
      - Be known as

Notes from one of
John's sermons.

IV. Come for the
Fruition experienced = - Realization
of Joy, Pleasure
= accomplished, fulfilled

A. Take my yoke; connection
  1. Reach out
  2. Faith & Trust
  3. Come

Jesus walks on water = says to
Peter "Come".
- sinks, but hand of Jesus
lifts him up

B. Learn - of me
  1. once for all
  not a casual contact, but constant, eternal
  like an eternal umbilical cord

  2. meek & lowly
    - incarnate = God in flesh
    - strong & understanding
    - gentle & mild

  3. a giver
    - life
    - blessing
    - eternal, heavenly realities on earth

  4. I am not like
    - Present Jewish, religious leaders
    - this present world
    - the greatest Prophet ever - John Baptist

- evil
- consuming
- selfish &
- religious

Paul the apostle

  5. I am
    - Son of the heavenly Father
    - the Coming One = Jn. Bapt. question
      - who enters your life experience
        - to change
        - empower
        - take your burden
        - give you rest

C. why?
  - to give to us
    - worth & dignity
    - security & significance
    - reality & fulfillment
    - Purpose & vision   - correct Priorities
    - heavenly & eternal
    - Salvation & glory

Jesus says, "Come to me," & you'll find
- Home to Father
- Home to our Creator
- Home to where all we are or hope to be, finds its life.

Then with no pastor, we had fill-in pastors for quite a few years. Then they wanted to make a pastor out of someone in the Gingrichs congregation. Abram (Abe) Hoover and I were both in the lot. I was washing the milkers, I'll never forget that, and the Lord said, "You're not going to be chosen, because I have other things for you to do." So I didn't even give it a thought. I went to the meeting where they had the lot, and I didn't even anticipate that I would get it. So Abe got it.

That's when I got the call from the Lord to work with the young people and develop Jubilee Ministries. Seven years later, Abe asked for help because the church was growing quite a bit. Merle Freed and I were chosen to be in the lot. At that time the Lord said, "You're going to be the minister; you're going to be chosen" just as clear as if somebody was there talking to me. So I had that confidence, and that's what happened. I got the book with the little slip of paper in it that said that I was chosen by God. That was in '77. February of '77 is when I was ordained.

JOHN LANDIS:
Family Counselor for Jubilee Family Ministries

John and his wife, Eileen, are the parents of five children. He co-pastors the Gingrich Mennonite Church as well as serving about one-third time as an itinerant evangelist. He can rightfully be called the founding father of Jubilee Ministries for God used his leadership efforts with the local youth group to establish a working relationship with the prison officials in the mid 1970's. His gifts of counseling, compassion and Bible exposition fit together well as he serves "on-call" with the distressed families who come to Jubilee for help.

You can't put two people or three people together in a team without a leader. You always have to have a leader. The bishop made a mistake, I think. He said Abe and I were co-leaders. I didn't like that; I don't think Abe liked it.

It became a difficult thing. Abe and I both felt very strongly about being the leader. Like I said, you need one person that's designated as leader and the other person needs to follow with and work along with, and hopefully they work together as a team. That wasn't really happening with Abe and I, and it was beginning to create some difficulties and problems.

I made the suggestion they free me half the time to go out and to teach and to preach, hold meetings, go to camp meetings, all kinds of things. They talked about it, and they gave me that privilege. So every other Sunday Gingrichs freed me to have meetings of some kind, either weekend or full week, or they could be revival meetings or teaching, almost anything I did. I enjoyed it.

That was formative for me. I got around to a lot of churches. I kept record of all the churches I spoke at until maybe the year 2000 or so. It was close to 200 different churches that I had meetings at, not just Mennonite, non-Mennonite as well. I taught at a lot of camps for the weeks of family camp or youth camp or different things like that. I really learned to know a lot of people, see a lot of churches, how they worked. It was a real learning experience for me.

1984

Jan-Feb.   Winter Bible School.   - Mechanic Grove, Palo Alto, Cedar Hill
                     Indiantown, Andrews Bridge, Kralls

2/4+5   • Camp Hebron - Manheim Couples Retreat

2/18   Sweet heart Banquet - Y.C.C.

3/30   New Covenant Banquet.

4/10   Hammer creek - Father-Son banquet

4/12   Cedar Crest "Who are the menn".

4/13-15   Black Rock
          Camp Hebron - marriage Retreat - (marriage Encounter) Eileen + J.

4/15   Blainsport. - Dating

4/21   Bowery mission N.Y.C. - Weaverland MYF

4/28   Vision For Witness at Harrisburg churches

5/3   Junior/Senior Banquet L.M.H.

5/11   L.M.H. Bd / Staff dinner

5/18   Evangelism Celebration at L.M.H.

5/27   Mexville 9:00am

6/2   L.M.H. Commencement

6/3   Chambersburg church - 9:00am. - "How to have W.B.S."

6/5   Manheim Christian School Commencement

6/16   Martindale - "Humble But Self Confident"

6/19-24   School of Apostles - Camp Black Rock

6/28   Camp Hebron - V.F.W. Spanish churches.

7/5   Giry - talk to Bible School teachers

7/6   Lost Creek. "Vision For Witness"

7/8   Metzlers

7/17   Giry - Amsterdam

7/21-28   Camp Hebron + Family Week "Relationships"

8/10-11   United Zion Young Couples Retreat - Their Camp grove.

8/25-26   Landis Family Retreat - Mt. Zion

9/8 +15   V.F.W. Seminar at Neffsville menn. church.

9/16 morning   Camp Hebron - Young Couples - Hornleys - Relationships

9/16 evening   Rawlingsville - Prison Experience

10/19   Glad Tidings Evang. Seminar - West Fallowfield -V.F.W.

10/20   Peace +Service Banquet "A Challenge of Service".

10/45   Giry - middle age martyrs

11/2-4   Peace Conference - Berne 2nd.

DOLAU BAPTIST CHURCH

Llanfihangel Rhydithon

invite you

to share in an evening of helpful

FELLOWSHIP

with

OUR FRIENDLY FARMER

JOHN LANDIS

from America

Tuesday 7 th June at 7.15 pm

John is the Pastor of a very large
CHRISTIAN CHURCH
in U.S.A. and th ... third
visit to D ... U

WE LOOK FORWARD TO SEEING YOU!

Ono United
Methodist Church

Will be hosting five evenings of special services

Wednesday, April 2 thru
Sunday, April 6

Our speaker will be

John G. Landis

Special music will be provided by local singer

Matthew J. Goss

Times: 7:00 each evening
Also 8:00 and 10:15 worship
services Sunday morning

Activities are also planned for children through
grade four at each service,
as well as nursery care for preschoolers.

A native of Lancaster county, John Landis was a dairy and cash crop farmer for 23 years, and then raised small fruits and vegetables for another eight years. While farming, Landis became involved in youth ministry. During this time, he had the privilege of starting Jubilee Ministries, an outreach to inmates and their families, in Lebanon. An ordained pastor in the Mennonite Church, Landis has been an evangelist and teacher in Pennsylvania, Maryland, Indiana, Belize, Canada and Wales. He taught Bible at Lancaster Mennonite High School, as well as counseling and teaching classes in the prison. He currently serves as a member of the Lebanon Rescue Mission Board. "I love the Lord and people. I have a desire that people experience the love and grace of God in every area of their

John preached, taught, and held special meetings in about 200 churches in the decade concluding with 2000. This notice invited the community in Wales to one of those services. Note it says this is the third time John had been at the Dolau Baptist Church.

John with the pastor of a church in Amsterdam, circa 1990s.

A lot of churches had two pastors. So I would be at the pastors' homes; I would be invited to both. They both would tell me their stories and difficulties that they had. It was information that was personal information. Their bishop didn't know it, Conference didn't know it. I wasn't free to unload to them either. I could have done a lot of help.

I did try to help men process their problems of who's the leader. That was the biggest thing of problems in leadership around the conference. Who's in charge? I don't know if that was ever settled. I know there were some that I had extended counseling that I did. I asked several years later, "How's it going?" and they said, "Well it's about the same." It left me know that it isn't a matter of the counseling and advice that's needed, it's a change of heart that's needed when you don't get along together.

That's something I worked at with Abe. Abe and I have an excellent relationship. We've had that for a long time. When I came to that time when I asked for extra time to go out and do things, the Lord spoke to me and said, "Let Abe be the leader. It isn't what the people wanted, but let Abe be the leader. Let him be in charge of it. You have something to do so go do it."

Hosting Bible study in the Landis family basement. They hosted Bible study in their home for 25 consecutive years.

After that Abe and I would have meetings together every week—and we were close, we got very close to each other. I'm glad for that. It was a good time for both of us to learn. I felt fulfilled. I saw a lot of good things happen in church, not only Gingrichs but in a lot of other churches in the district as well.

I don't have many regrets about things. If I could redo a couple things, I would, but I can't do that, so it's a matter of learning from it and taking care of your feelings and their feelings. I feel good about where everything's at. At peace.

So it went a few years and I had started Jubilee Ministries, it was going well. The congregation wanted to have a full-time pastor, and I was chosen to do that. I was farming a big operation at that time—several hundred acres—which isn't big today.

Abe was ten years older than me. I still considered him a partner with me, even though I was the one chosen to be salaried. It's a difference in being a salaried pastor from being a free ministry, as they call it. There seems to be an ownership when they start to pay you, that they have rights to tell you what to do and how much you can do. That happened at Gingrichs.

The church was still growing. We had added an educational wing and the big narthex. We fixed up the basement for meals and things like that, and we were reaching out through various things in the district. We were looked to, pretty much, as a growing and leadership church. That was all good and well.

While farming, pastoring, and raising a family, John's sermon prep times sometimes necessarily started with a little nap, here at the kitchen table in farmhouse on Thompson Avenue, circa mid 1980s when John was also teaching at Lancaster Mennonite School.

With my work ethic that I have, and with the good ol' work ethic that all my people there at Gingrichs had, they wanted me to keep track of the hours I put in, even though I was salaried. That was interesting.

In 1978 I left the dairy farm, sold out to a young man, and bought the 23 acre farm back here. We went into the small fruit and vegetable business. So I was still farming. The salary Gingrichs paid was not enough to live on, and so I still had to have income.

For a while I worked at Fontana Steel as their mechanic and maintenance person, guess I did four and a half years there. That was interesting, too—a teaching experience for me. I learned a lot of things about steel and manufacturing and being a mechanic and keeping everybody happy.

I spent one year at Lancaster Bible College learning Greek. I took a few other classes that I didn't have time to

Some of the ways Eileen ministered alongside John was through teaching Sunday school, which she had done since she was a young person, and through hospitality.

Eileen and John teaching Gingrichs Mennonite Church children about the elements of communion with a bread-making demonstration.

take for credit, but I took Greek for credit. That was a challenge. It helped me to write things not like a farmer. I learned to write a little more in a specific form of English, which I could never quite understand. One time I said to my Greek professor at Lancaster Bible College, "You know it's interesting how you're teaching me how every writer who wrote in the Bible wrote according to their own individual personality. Now here you want me to follow your personality!" He didn't like that. I'm the kind of fellow that I'm not ashamed or afraid to give opposing viewpoints. I always enjoyed that in college.

The reason I didn't move on then is because Lancaster Mennonite High School came after me to take Glen Sell's place as Bible teacher there. I said, "Well, I guess I can do that." We had three children attending there, and it would help to lower their tuition. So I taught for three years at LMH. I enjoyed that. I brought not just the ability to be able to tell stories, but stories of meaning. I had a student at the end of one semester who said to me, "Mr. Landis, do you know how many stories you told this semester?" "No, I don't." She said, "237 stories."

But by the end of my third year of teaching, school Superintendent Dick Thomas said that I should have a degree to continue teaching. I had a high rating with all the students and parents, but I didn't have a degree.

John teaching bible at Lancaster Mennonite High School, which he did 1983—1986.

John G. Landis' Morning Prayer

I am crucified with Christ:
nevertheless I live;
yet not I, but Christ liveth in me:
and the life which I now live in the flesh
I live by the faith of the Son of God,
who loved me, and gave himself for me.
But God forbid that I should glory,
save in the cross of our Lord Jesus Christ,
by whom the world is crucified unto me,
and I unto the world.
And this I pray,
That your love may abound yet more and
    more
in knowledge and in all judgment;
That you may approve things that are
    excellent;
that you may be sincere and without offense
till the day of Christ;
Being filled with the fruits of righteousness,
which are by Jesus Christ, unto the glory
    and praise of God.

Galatians 2:20 and 6:14, Philippians 1:9–11

They wanted every teacher to have a teaching degree, and I didn't have that. I had attended a lot of different colleges, I did correspondence courses, attended several seminaries and did courses. But I only took what I wanted, a course at a time, over a period of time. Nobody wanted to give me any credit for that, so I don't have a degree for teaching. I don't know if it would have helped me at all in that. I still have students from that era that reflect back and say, "You helped to change my life." It wasn't because of a degree, but because the Lord used me for his own advantage in these individual lives.

Those were good years, very good years.

Jubilee Ministries

Describing the beginnings of Jubilee is a big story! Like I said earlier, I was involved in youth work, in leadership at Landis Valley before I was married. I always liked youth; it seemed like youth and I got along good together. I was the youth leader for the Lebanon district of Lancaster Mennonite Conference prior to the 1968 division.

When the division came, the bishops appointed me to be in charge of the youth that stayed with Lancaster Conference. That became a very large group of young people because there happened to be a lot of youth in these churches. I think at several of the first meetings we had, we had 60 to 80 youth attending youth meetings. That's unusual.

I worked at the whole idea of spiritual growth and at numerical growth. One night we were meeting in the basement of Elmer Martin's home—where his

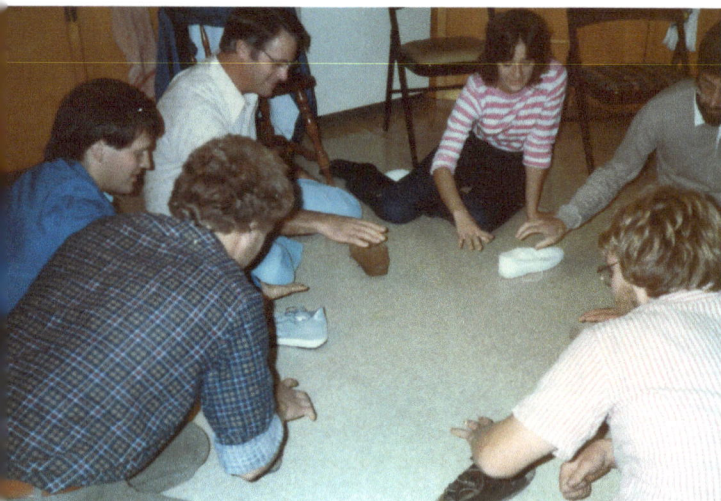

John playing "the shoe game" with youth from Lebanon District of Lancaster Mennonite Conference in the kitchen of the Thompson Avenue farmhouse. Left to right: Larry Groff, Yost Landis (friend of Larry from Germany who lived with John and Eileen for a year), John Landis, Shelley Martin, Dan Gehman, unidentified friend of Yost.

Youth activity: a 1960s taffy pull.

son Robert Martin lives today—we had our youth meetings there. We'd have 40, 50, 60, sometimes up to 90 packed into that basement for the Bible studies and prayer that we had every week for the youth. They'd come from Hammer Creek, from all over Lancaster County. Great young people.

One night in a time of expressing viewpoints and sharing views and that kind of thing, a young lady tapped me on the shoulder, said, "I'd like to talk with you." I said, "Okay." I had prayer and a closing and dismissed the youth, then she and I went over to the corner of the basement, and she confessed immorality. I prayed with her. I said, "Would you like to share—not what you did—but what just happened here in your life?" She said, "Yeah."

Some youth had already left, but this young lady gave her testimony of peace because of confession of sin to the 42 young people still there. I said to them, "Let's gather around this young lady and pray for her." I'm a strong believer in prayer, and I tried to teach them that. That prayer time didn't stop until about 1:30 in the morning!

It was a filling of the Holy Spirit. I had gone through some things myself, and I had that infilling. He just came in powerful ways. Those youth were changed. Not all of them, maybe, but most of the youth had an infilling of the Holy Spirit that they never had before.

I started to get telephone calls from parents: "What'd you do to my son? What'd you do to my daughter?" Pastors called and said, "What'd you do to our young people?" "Why are you asking that?" "Well they're different."

And they were, they were fireballs. They went out on their own—two by twos, or threes—and would

Business card as Youth Service Counselor to advise young men on their options for the draft for the Vietnam War, circa 1969.

```
YOUR YOUTH SERVICE COUNSELOR
for the Lebanon District

John G. Landis
R.D. 4
Lebanon, Pa. 17042

(717)-867-1517

Directions: One mi. south of
Annville on Rt 934 turn left
at Granger's Provisions, go
one mile to my home.
```

give out tracts, visit places the whole way up to Pine Grove, east toward Hamburg, all around Lebanon County. They were just on fire for the Lord. It was amazing. I had never experienced this before in a group.

I sensed the Lord saying, "Pull them together again and give them some training. Give them some teaching, develop some leadership." And I did. Amazing what God did. Out of that group of people have come college professors with their PhDs, have come doctors, have come businessmen, have come pastors, even women pastors!

I had a couple young ladies in that group who were fireballs before the Holy Spirit had come, and it wasn't necessarily in the best way. They'd challenge me just to pick up an interesting discussion. One of them, who is still a professor at Eastern Mennonite University, told me "How you influenced us, I don't know, but you really did a good job." I said, "You really got too much education, if you don't know how that happened!"

Some of the young people went to the Lebanon prison and knocked on that door. The prison said, "You can't come in." So the youth came back to me and said, "Pray that the prison doors will open" and "can you do it?" I said, "Tell you what I'll do. I'll go visit the prison board and see what's open."

So I did, I went to an evening meeting of the prison board. I asked them just three questions: What do they want us to do? What can we do? What do we have to do to be ready to do something? I never got so laughed at, so mocked, so pounded down as that evening. These were fellows that probably didn't have much understanding of Mennonites, and they didn't understand much about God and the Bible.

I sat there after it was over. The meeting was dismissed, everyone was leaving. There was a fellow there, Big Jim Whitman—that's what everyone called him— Big Jim Whitman, and he was the probation officer for juveniles. I knew him, and he came over and laid his hand on my shoulder, he said, "John, you really stirred the pot tonight. I don't want you to quit. You've begun something that's going to be good." I said, "Thanks, Jim. I needed that before I go out of this building." Another thing that Jim said, he said, "John, the next time don't come to this board. Go right in and talk to the warden." I didn't know the warden.

I did a lot of praying, and I drew up a program of possible things we could do within the prison, as young people, as youth. So I called ahead of time, and then I went into the prison. When I got to the door, they left me in and took me right to the warden's office. Warden Wike. Short, stocky Italian. No nonsense, but a kind guy. When I came into his office he had his feet propped up on the desk and was smoking a black stogie. We chit chatted some to get to know each other, and then he said, "What do you want, John?"

I took my paper and laid it in front of him. He shifted the stogie to the other side of his mouth, took it, and read through it. "Why do you want to do this?" I told him, I said, "There's a couple reasons and one is I have a group of young people who are on fire for the Lord that want to serve." (He was a Catholic, he knew what I was talking about.) "They'd like to serve in the prison in some form," which I had put there on that paper. I said, "I have full confidence that they will do a good job and that you can appreciate their being there."

He took the stogie out, punched it out on the ashtray, looked at me and said, "When can you begin?" You talk about the Lord opening doors! I said, "Give us two weeks." He said, "Okay." He wrote it down on his pad.

Amazing, amazing. When I went back to the youth, they were wondering what happened, so I told them. It went like fire through the whole youth group.

We started with a Bible study and singing. I suggested to the youth that we include the prison in our softball league. They bought that up, just like that, and the prison became one of the teams of the softball league that we had among our churches. Well, that opened doors. They would bring these prisoners out on a stake body truck, standing in the back of the truck. That stuff wouldn't pass today.

Warden Wike and I became good friends. I really appreciated him. I asked him to point out prisoners he thought I should talk to. We had brought some counselors along, too. It started to make a difference. They knew there was a difference, a change in the prison. They couldn't deny it. Wike told me "You are making a difference."

Youth from a community church pray before a game.

The outreach was growing to witness out on the streets. It was an exciting time. I had a core of youth leaders, about seven of them, and I told them "I think we need more help, and we need to organize differently. This is getting beyond you." They right away picked up on it and said, "Yes, we want to go to the district leadership. We want them to back us and to give finances to pay the bills of things that we're buying." I said, "Okay, I'll make an appeal to them." I did.

I ended up heading up a committee that studied the situation, answered the district's questions, and they blessed us to form an organized group. The first part of it was under the Mennonite Valley Youth Fellowship title, but it wasn't long till we had our own title: Jubilee Ministries, Inc. We were incorporated. A board was formed for this organization.

Left to right: Victor Ziegler, Ed Arnold, and John Landis at the annual Jubilee meeting at Gingrichs Mennonite Church, circa late 1970s. Victor was a Jubilee board member, Mr. Arnold was on the Lebanon County Prison Board, and John chaired the Jubilee board of directors. Many of the women seen here worked in the Jubilee thrift shop.

We started to get invitations. Philhaven invited us to go to their halfway house in Palmyra. And then we formed a halfway house.

The women from the Lebanon district came to us when I was chairman of the board and chairman of Jubilee Ministries. The women said, "Can't we have some way of running a Re-Uz-It shop or something? We'll staff it, we'll run it, the whole nine yards, whatever there is to do." I told the two ladies that came to me, "Put down who you are, how you would run it, and how you would finance it, and then bring it to our board." They brought it to the next board meeting. They were on the ball. They had everything all figured out. They had a lawyer to help them put it together. It would be under the Jubilee board. That's how the Jubilee thrift stores started.

Everything that Jubilee does comes out of that whole birthing of thrift stores, of that beginning. Everything. It's between a two- to three-million dollar operation right now. It runs a lot of programs. There are five stores. I had told them that I would stay as chairman in charge of things until we got in the black, until everything was settled, leadership was trained and all of that. It was about seven years, I think, something like that. They've got some exciting visions that they'd like to do things in the future. To me it's been a multi-colored blessing of seeing God work from the ground up, the whole way. It's been beautiful; it's been wonderful. If God wants to do something, he will do it.

That first summer after we had had the renewal, the Lebanon Recreation Department asked me whether we as the youth could take over five summer playgrounds and run their programs. I said, "Let me try." I said, "We're not organized yet to be able to do that, but let me see if I can put something together."

I went to Salunga to the Mission Board. I thought we could tie this in with their Voluntary Service program. I thought it was excellent. Well, they didn't have that viewpoint. I tried a couple other things, and I came up empty-handed in everything that I wanted. I didn't get any help. You get disappointments in life, too.

I talked to Jerry Higley, who was chairman and man in charge of Youth for Christ. In a sense he bought into my vision. They are now working really well in organizing things for the children and youth of Lebanon County, particularly Lebanon city, which is a beautiful thing. I support them 100%; I think they are just wonderful that they are doing that.

I had one or two other things that I had tried to take to our Mennonite organizations. If you're not a part of it, and you don't have power in it, or you don't have a lot of money, you ain't getting anywhere. Pardon me. But that's what I ran up against. So there were some disappointing things, too.

I told Clair Weaver, who became the person that was the program director and CEO for Jubilee, "I just want you to know this. I had told the Lord from the beginning that we'll give him all the glory, all the credit for everything. I have confidence that he'll bless this as long as he gets the credit and the glory." So when Clair handed it over to the new man who's now been in for three years, I guess, that message got passed along to him. "This is a ministry of the Lord, for the Lord, and to the Lord for the people. We're not a church." So it's pretty well kept that up.

Now it has not just Mennonites on the board: there's one of the county judges was on the board, there's businessmen on the board, there's all kinds of denominations on the board.

There's even some thought of expanding, reaching out, and joining another organization. I served on the Lebanon Rescue Mission board for twenty-some years also. I dropped a hint some time ago—maybe ten years ago—that these two organizations are reaching the same people, doing the same things, is there any way we can hook them together and do it better and do more? It hasn't developed yet. They're still talking about it. I expect that might in some form happen. I personally believe it needs to happen, but that's me.

Growing Other Ministries

I was involved in many other ministries over the years, often in a leadership role. With Camp Hebron, that was a time of life of growth for me. It was also a time of reaching people that I wouldn't have reached any other way, of seeing things happen.

The first three years that I was co-leader of Camp Hebron Family Camp—Bill Weaver was co-leader with me—that thing grew to 380-some people. Camp Hebron people came to me and wondered if they couldn't start another camp. So we started another family camp the next year, and that grew.

John enjoyed leading family camps at Camp Hebron, Halifax, PA, for a number of years.

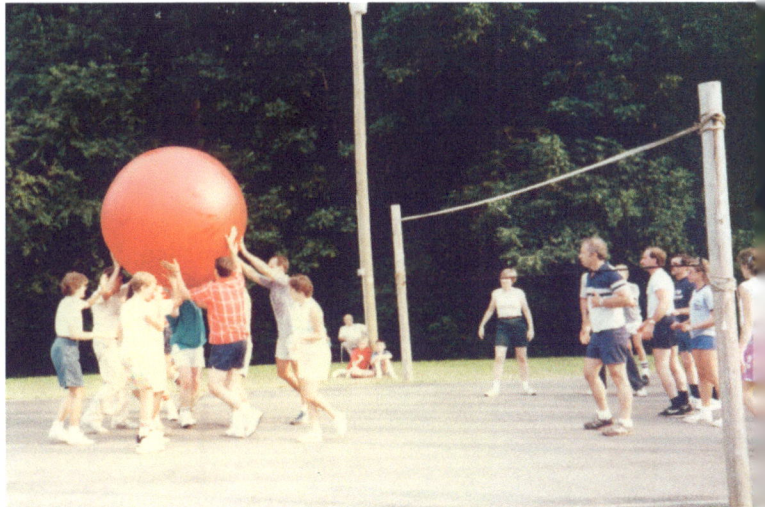

I don't know how many family camps they have now, but during the eight years I was involved it grew to three family camps. That was a blessing to see that happening. They all formed kind of their own character and personality, because they were all a bit different. I enjoyed that.

I was asked by the director of the Rescue Mission, Bill Coleman, whether I would be interested in being a part of the board. For me all these things were growth experiences. It was a time of helping an organization develop better leadership—have a bigger vision, and attempt to fulfill that vision—for all those organizations: for Jubilee, for Camp Hebron, for Lebanon Rescue Mission.

Bill Coleman, at the Rescue Mission, was a wonderful man. He was older than I am now, and he was loved by everybody. He wasn't too much on growing the Rescue Mission because the facilities couldn't handle any more. We had meals together often, Bill and I did.

After Bill wrapped up as director, the board tried to connect with Jubilee. But we had a director at that point, of the Rescue Mission, that wanted no ties to Jubilee. He was going to build something for his own name's sake. Pardon me in saying that, but that's what it amounted to. But we had laid the seed in the ground for that to happen. So I'm expecting that's going to happen sometime in the future here.

The Rescue Mission has grown: they have another facility, they have a big facility. They continue to expand their ministry. They have a very good director, a woman, and I have high respect for her. I told her that when she was finally chosen. I said, "The Lord is going to do great things through you." She just looked at me. She was a single lady at the time, and she was in her 40s, her 50s. She said, "You really believe that, John?" I said, "I do. You've got the ability, you've got the leadership skills, you have the vision. You have everything's that needed." And she has been guiding it very well, very well.

They have two good leaders now—one from Jubilee, one from the Rescue Mission—and they are meeting together to talk about this. But these Dutchmen up here, it's hard to move them. The board for the Lebanon Rescue Mission is made up of all good Dutchmen. And so are the board members for Jubilee. So they have a couple pretty good size hills or mountains to cross. But if the Lord wants it, it'll happen.

In the midst of all this, a couple men came to me and wondered whether I would help them start a church school. I said, "Lord, why now?"

I have a strong viewpoint on church schools and on Christians in public schools. I'm a strong proponent of Christians being Christians in public school. I really believe that. Our children all graduated from a church school, except one. That was Darryl, our oldest, who did not transfer from public school to Lancaster Mennonite until his junior year. But they all went to public school too, then ended up in a church school to finish up.

My viewpoint made me think, why do we need a church school? These two gentlemen said, "Well think about it." And I did. I prayed. I decided I would work with them. I said, "I don't want to be a principal or chief person in getting this established. I have my plate full enough. But I will sit with you, I will talk with you, I will encourage you, I will give you ideas." They said, "Well, that's all we need."

Some of them were Church of the Brethren, some of them were other denominations. They wanted a Christian school, not necessarily a Mennonite school, which is what New Covenant Christian School is. Sure

Eileen and John enjoying relaxed time at Diener's Restaurant, along Route 30 in Lancaster.

enough, they got it off the ground. Started with 20 or 30 students, I think today there's just about 300. They have a building program that's going, in process. So that, again, is another thing that I knew that the Lord's blessing was on, and he has been directing.

I served on the New Covenant Christian School board for 12 years, and then I went off the board. Then things got ferhutzed, so I was asked to come back on the board again. I left them know it was only a two or three year assignment for me. So they got things pulled together, and it's going well.

When you have a leadership that doesn't have the vision, doesn't have the Holy Spirit in the same form, you're not going to grow, you're not going to push the walls out. That's what one of the problems was. We had I don't know how many different denominations that sent their children there. So there was this whole, you know, "they don't quite believe like we do" attitude. Fact is, I don't know if there's any Mennonite kids going there now. I don't know. That bothers me.

I have over the years become a staunch Mennonite who is very open for the beliefs of other people. There's a lot of fine Christians that aren't Mennonites. Some Mennonites I would like to see more Christian.

I am open to listening and to working with others. Gingrichs Mennonite physically sits in the center between Mormons and Jehovah's Witnesses. There's three churches in a row there. I was always open to listening to them and to dialoguing with them. They don't have the complete truth. It's sad. They've got the zeal but not the right truth. That's important. Of course it happens to Mennonites, too.

On Leadership

How did I learn to lead, and who were my mentors? Sometimes it was a matter of who did I observe and *didn't* want to lead like that. That was some of it. I think sometimes leadership is a gift. Some of it came naturally.

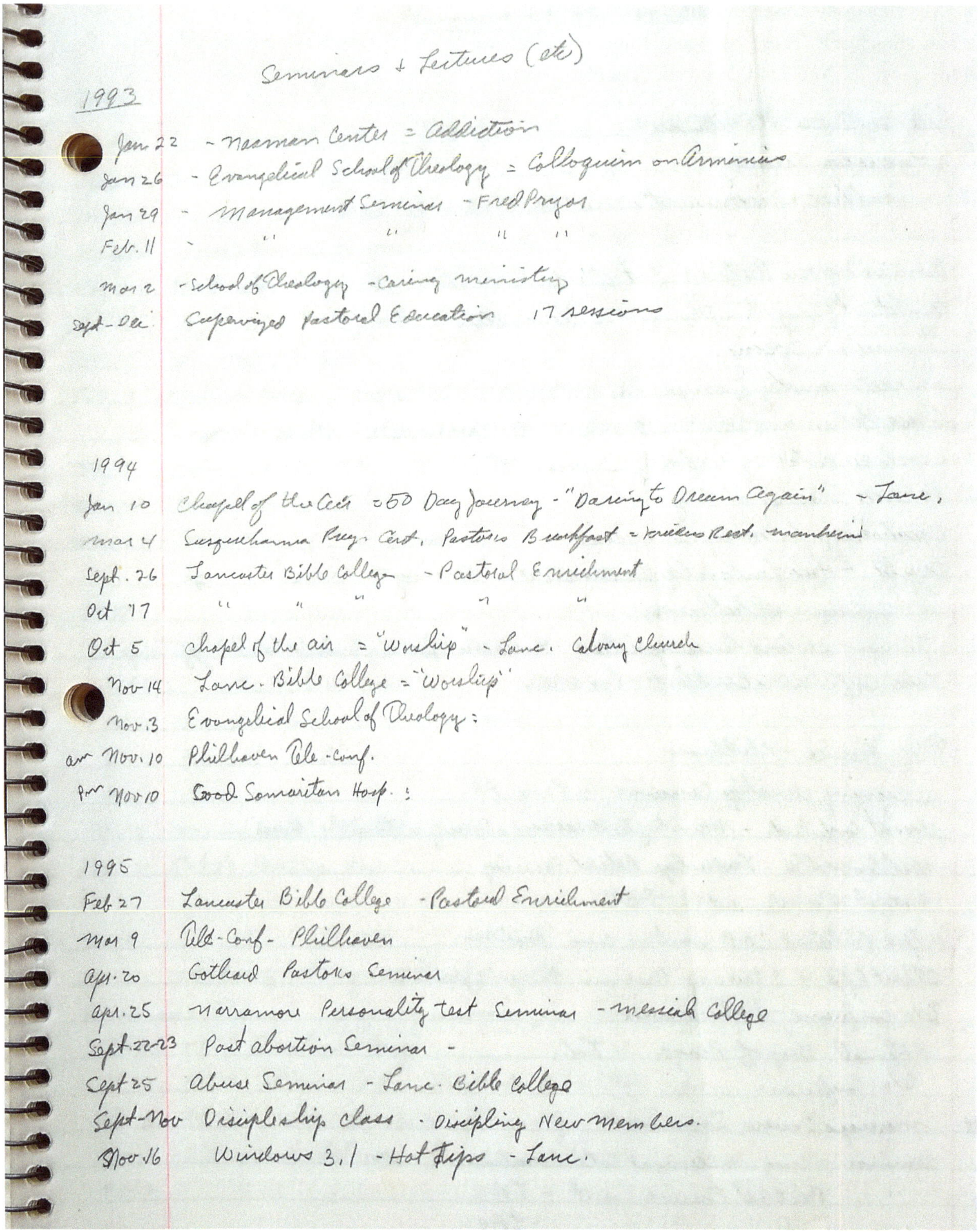

Seminars + Lectures (etc)

_1993_

Jan 22 – Naaman Center = Addiction

Jan 26 – Evangelical School of Theology = Colloquium on Arminius

Jan 29 – Management Seminar – Fred Pryor

Feb. 11 – " " " "

Mar 2 – School of Theology – caring ministry

Sept–Dec Supervised Pastoral Education 17 sessions

_1994_

Jan 10 Chapel of the Air = 50 Day Journey – "Daring to Dream Again" – Lanc.

Mar 4 Susquehanna Prog. Cent. Pastors Breakfast = Krules Rest. Manheim

Sept. 26 Lancaster Bible College – Pastoral Enrichment

Oct 17 " " " "

Oct 5 Chapel of the air = "Worship" – Lanc. Calvary Church

Nov 14 Lanc. Bible College = "Worship"

Nov. 3 Evangelical School of Theology :

am Nov. 10 Philhaven Tele-conf.

pm Nov 10 Good Samaritan Hosp. :

_1995_

Feb 27 Lancaster Bible College – Pastoral Enrichment

Mar 9 Tele-Conf – Philhaven

Apr. 20 Gotland Pastors Seminar

Apr. 25 Narramore Personality test Seminar – Messiah College

Sept. 22–23 Post abortion Seminar –

Sept 25 Abuse Seminar – Lanc. Bible College

Sept–Nov Discipleship class · Discipling New Members.

Nov 16 Windows 3.1 – Hot tips – Lanc.

John has been a lifelong learner, taking advantage of seminars and education on a variety of topics.

I enjoy history, and I enjoy reading. Some of it has come from reading biographies or autobiographies or stories of missionaries, stories of political leaders, of generals, of businessmen. I'm an avid reader. There's two big shelves in my library: one is on leadership and the other's on psychology and counseling. I always have my ears tuned to people that can speak wisdom. I think that's been a tremendous help to me.

I'd sign up for a two-day or a three-day seminar on a certain kind of leadership or certain business styles or how to do things, but in general I didn't learn leadership in the classroom. I don't seem to fit well in classrooms that a professor or a teacher wants to make a fool out of somebody. I've been in those.

There's a sense in me that can read people. I often quote Fred Smith, who is founder of Federal Express. He said, "There's too many leaders today that have risen to the level of their incompetence." That is true. I can pick it out of a bishop, a preacher, a deacon or just somebody that's organizing things. They shouldn't be there, but they are.

I can pretty well sense if somebody's going to make it or not make it. I don't take that credit to myself, that's of the Lord. That's something he has given to me in a natural, spiritual sense. I do a lot of reflecting.

Coming to the mentors and people that mentored for me: Lancaster Conference Bishop David Thomas, I had mentioned him before, he was a model for me. On being a teacher, J. Irvin Lehman from Franklin County. He was an excellent teacher. There were people that I watched, watched their lives, watched how they did things.

I had been talking to David Thomas and to some other bishops about leadership training for the Conference. I helped to get a couple leadership classes started in that, and a college professor from Eastern Mennonite College (now University), and I were co-teaching this one class.

This guy's a PhD, he's written books, he's been well-known over the conferences, he taught at Elkhart, Indiana too. He said to me, "John, you seem frustrated when you're up there." I said, "Yeah, can you guess why?" He said, "Well, it's probably the same thing that I'm frustrated about. They want us to say things a certain way, don't they?" I said, "Yeah, they want us to come out where they come out."

He asked, "Is that the way you find life?" I said, "No, it isn't. These canned programs are for the individual that produced them, not for the people that are studying them." "You're right, he said. "Why don't we just do what we want to do? We'll deal with it tonight after it's over." I told him, "Okay, I'm all for it. You're going first, remember!" And we did.

Conference leadership acted as though they couldn't understand why we wouldn't take what they had produced and make it work. What's the matter with it? Boy, he laid into them. He could do that. I couldn't. He was about two years older than me, something like that, and he was well known in the church.

"I always have my ears turned to people that . . . speak wisdom."

John G. Landis.

Experience also—if you're a learner, experience becomes a great thing. I think that's one thing that we have lost in relation to teaching children. When something happens a certain way, that's a teaching moment. What are you learning out of it? I think of the time when I was teaching at Lancaster Mennonite High School, and I had time for the students to give reflections about what they were going through. I used those as stepping stones, and they appreciated it.

My dad was a good leader, and he led by example. I did the exact same thing in my parenting. My dad didn't just send us out to the field to hoe weeds or pull weeds or do something, my dad took us out. That's the way I did with our boys. I would take them out to hoe weeds, to pull weeds, to pick strawberries, to pick asparagus, to pick raspberries, to load the wagons. I left my boys drive the tractor. I worked, and they knew that.

I experienced that when I worked at Fontana Steel as their head mechanic and maintenance fellow. We went down to the docks at Philly, and we dropped two big bridge cranes, which are cranes that are on top of dollies that have railroad car wheels on them and run on a track up and down. They have a crane connection underneath that picks up whatever needs picking up.

The boss was going to be in charge of things. The first one we were working on, he did something wrong and almost got killed. He turned it all over to me. "It's yours, John. Get them down, take them home." I had to do some fast thinking. I didn't send the men to do the most dangerous things; I went there and I helped them do it, or I did it.

Now here's the punchline at the end of this story. We had taken a crane down, and we had set it to bring these things up and down or down and up. We had to take some bracing loose from the roof to get the crane up far enough to have the right angle to work the cables. So when we had everything down, we were cleaning up, and somebody was going to have to go up there on that crane—walk up the crane arm—and put those brackets back on and weld them fast.

I started up, and I heard this fellow call me, "John, don't you go up there. I'll go up." I had a group of 18–19 year olds who worked for me down there, about six of them. This one guy who was a really rowdy, rough character, he said, "I don't want you going up there." I said, "Why not?" He said, "You got a wife and children at home. I don't have anybody but my parents and brothers and sisters. I'm going up." I just looked at him. I said, "Are you sure?" He said, "I'm sure. Get down here." Why did he do that?

I met him here a couple years ago. He was working in Lebanon on a big building. He said, "John, do you remember the time down at Philly at the docks?" I said, "Yeah. I don't know if I ever thanked you, but you don't know how relieved I was when you took my place to go up there and weld that steel back together." He said, "I'm glad I did. You changed my life." Wow.

So we talked. I hadn't recognized him because he had long hair now, and he had a full beard. But it really touched me. I said, "Why did you do it?" He said, "You were involved in every bit of what we did. You took our place many times. You didn't send us to do it. You did it, or you helped us."

It's too much the case that we think leadership is telling people what to do. That's not leadership. Leadership is walking the way and doing it. How do I know that? Look at Jesus. He's my supreme example. That's exactly what he did.

My Greek teacher at Lancaster Bible College is another man that set a pretty good example for me and showed a lot of empathy and good will toward me. I was the "old man" when I took Greek. You should take Greek when you're younger! He told me that, then he said, "I'll work with you."

The morning that I was going to take the final test in Greek, I had, down here on the farm, eight acres of strawberries that were in full bloom, and it was to be frosty that morning. I had left early to get down to school, and frost would come right after the sun would rise. I had nobody but Eileen—says a lot about Eileen—to start up the irrigation equipment if the temperature dropped below freezing. She had to start it and make sure that it was all connected. During my test I could not think Greek for anything.

The teacher was collecting the papers, and said, "You don't have anything written down." I said, "I'm sorry, I just can't think Greek." I told him why not. He looked at me, he said, "John, go for a walk." He had me literally get up and go for a walk and start thinking Greek. He said, "When you get back here, I'll give you your test back."

I didn't do real good, I did a C. He looked at me and said, "You're better than what that shows." So he gave me a better final grade. That is the kind of thing we need today.

On Monday I sat with a new bishop. He wanted to meet with me, talk with me. He has great ideas. I didn't have time to really point some things out that he needs to take into consideration. He's well-degreed, well-studied. But he still hasn't been through the mill!

Travel, Preach, Teach, and Learn

John: I responded to invitations to preach and teach in many different countries.

I had quite an experience in Canada one February. I was invited through Northern Youth Ministries to work with their teachers and to teach the workers. That was a cold experience, very cold. First ten days I was in 30-degrees-below-zero weather. I slept in a cabin that had no heat. I slept with my shoes on, my overcoat on to stay warm enough to sleep.

During the day I held meetings in a luxurious open area, the narthex, of a big dormitory that they had for women. At night in the men's cabin, there was no room even on the floor. I said something about sleeping on one of the sofas or one of the big chairs in the meeting room. I could have been warm. They said, "No, we can't let you be with the women." None of the workers invited me to their homes, which I didn't understand.

Next I went up above the Arctic Circle with them, to the farthest north that they were. It was cold! We drove 12 hours, and it was that cold the car never gave any heat out of the heater.

I didn't know this, but there were two girls up there that used to be in my youth group. We got there about midnight and boy, I tell you, it was good old Lancaster County-Lebanon County hospitality. They had beef stew on the stove and warm drinks: coffee, cocoa. They had put out a heating iron—had two of them in my bed—so that the bed would be warm. And I had heat in my bedroom. I told those girls, "Oh my goodness, you are spoiling me. I haven't had anything like this the last ten days!" So I was treated nice there.

They took me to an airport then, backwoods airport, and flew me out to Thunder Bay in a small plane. I was going to get on another plane in Thunder Bay, but I had to layover one day. The ministry had contacted one of their homes there on the outskirts of Thunder Bay. I think it was three miles out, something like that. Said when I'd be there.

When I got there, I did something that I don't do anymore. I paid the taxi and let them go before I knew I was getting in the door. Would you believe it, the lady in charge was not home. I couldn't get in. Those girls who lived at the home would not let me in, and it was 35 or more below zero. I was walking with my suitcase. I walked down the street a while and come back and knocked on the door again. They said, "No, mister. We can't let you in, and she's not here yet."

Hypothermia—my body was wearing down. When I went back the last time, I had my mind made up that if they cracked that door, I'm breaking in. I knocked. The girls said to the lady—she was there, believe it or not—that there's this man that says he's supposed to stay here and just keeps bugging us.

I heard her scream. She grabbed that door, yanked it open, reached out—she was a big woman—grabbed me by the coat in the front, pulled me in. Told one of the girls, "Go start filling the tub with water." She was giving them orders. She yanked the clothes off of me, pulled my shoes off, took me and pushed me in that water. I tell you, I was close to dying of the cold weather. It also put the period to the sense that I'm not coming back to this place anymore!

Yearly over a four-year period Eileen and I spent the month of June in Wales through Glen Sell's Gateway Evangelistic Ministry. That was a blessing. We knew Glen and Ethel Sell before. So that was great. They had a lot of friends in Wales.

Eileen: I enjoyed that—being in another culture, learning. We were always hosted by a minister and his wife over there. Learning the different ways different people do things. That was fun.

We'd take three days during the four weeks and hop the English Channel and go to Holland and minister there. That was all set up through Bob and Mim Phillips, a couple that we loved dearly at Gingrichs and then blessed to go to Holland. Holland is interesting. Very intelligent people, beautiful people. But a sense of spirituality? Not much. Not much.

When we were at Billy Graham's evangelism conference in Amsterdam in '83—Eileen and I—the hotel that we stayed in was right next to the red light section. Every morning and every evening, we'd see the same thing. There would be stacks of beer cans that would be 15-20 foot long, stacked, cans side by side, on a pyramid 6-7 feet high, and they'd be empty in the morning. The city would come around, clean up the beer cans. By evening, they'd be stacked up again. People drunk everywhere. It was so pathetic.

Glen and Ethel Sell, Eileen and John Landis.

1983, Amsterdam, Netherlands, Billy Graham's International Conference for Itinerant Evangelists. Glen Sell and John Landis participated in workshops during the conference.

With friends at the conference. Left to right: Eileen Landis, Glen Sell, Ethel Sell, and unidentified attendees.

Same way, the red light section was horrible. Nude people. So that conference was a real enlightenment for us, too. Being with Bob and Mim and seeing what they faced and how they were starting a church and how it was going. They needed a lot of encouragement, so we tried to give that. Then we'd fly back to Heathrow Airport at London to fly out to come home.

In Wales we learned that a sheep does not say "baa." No, it goes, "maaa, maaaa!"

I don't know if we could thank Glen and Ethel and their whole board enough. They more than paid our way. We saw changes in people, saw good things in Wales, and saw things that broke our heart. I often wonder how those churches are doing now. It was a great time of fellowship with people, a great challenge.

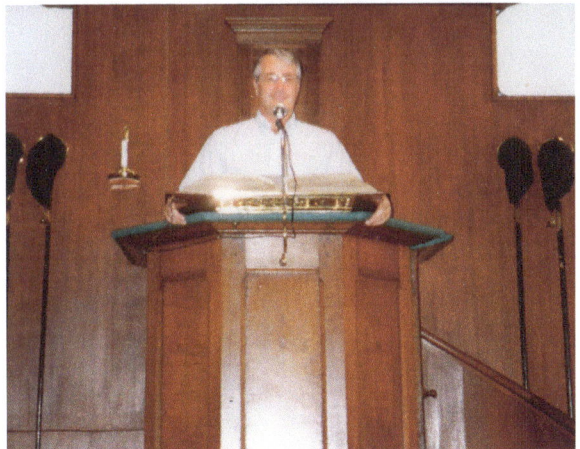

John preaching at a church in Wales.

One night in a country church—a big, stone church maybe the size of East Petersburg Mennonite, and of course they had the pulpit up in the wall—I went up into the pulpit, and I knew there was a thunderstorm coming. We had a "boom," and the lights went out. The pastor said, "Keep on preaching, John." It was dark; I had no light. I preached everything from memory and the Spirit.

The first church that I was at on Sunday morning—it was a large church, too, a Reformed church, sat up on a hill—the deacon in charge, he gave me a piece of paper and said, "Here's the order of the service. Let's pray." Well, I could hardly understand his writing, and I had never been at a Welsh service before. I didn't know the order. I couldn't read his writing.

So I went up the round circular thing up to the pulpit, where I could look straight into the balcony. I looked to one side and saw the organist was in back of me, and she was sitting there with a fur coat on, had herself all bundled up sitting at the organ. She was looking at me, so I looked at the paper. That's a number I can read! So I gave the number of the song out—why the deacon didn't say something then, I don't know.

I had been told that they always read the first verse of the hymn. I read the first verse, and the deacon says, "Mister. That's the wrong number!" He gave the number, and so then I turned to that one, I apologized, and read the first verse. I thought, John, do your thing and keep going. Don't quit. You're in charge.

This big church didn't have enough people to pay for heating bills. They had three or four heating registers along the side and I don't know how many benches in between. That's where people were sitting, at the ends of their benches, at those registers. That's how cold it was in there.

Wonderful people. I talked to them, had fun with them, though I didn't know any of the words. You learn a lot when you realize that hey, you don't know as much as you think you do! That was a wonderful experience working with Glen and Ethel.

We got invited to Belize by a young lady who lived not too far from us growing up and I knew personally. She had married a German settlement Mennonite man in Belize. She remembered me in teaching, and she invited me down there for their youth conference.

Belize is an English colony, and so they spoke English. Very good English, British English. It was different. I never saw bugs with nothing but mouths that could bite so bad as they did! Sand mites they called them. You couldn't see them except if the sun was coming in the window, then it looked like dust. But it was all sand mites. Oh, could they bite!

Her husband picked us up and took us to their home. We slept at their home one night. He was a Mennonite businessman. He and his family and brothers had developed a chicken business in Belize. They had chickens that laid eggs that they hatched for broilers. They built the business for people in Belize to have jobs. It amazing to watch how they shipped several thousand chickens every day, that they had butchered, and they put them out on the market. The chickens were grown by Belizean people. It gave them something to earn an income with.

The Belizean people out in the bush are very poor. We went out to this camp. Talk about driving through back country and bumpy roads and potholes and you

John preaching in Belize. Interpreter, Roman, standing to John's left listening intently.

Eileen making a pup tent a home. This where she and John slept during their weeks of ministering in Belize during August 1985. The camp site was in a cow pasture, with cows roaming the pasture at night.

name it. We got to this place they called a camp. Actually, it was a farm. They had put a sun shield up of palm and banana leaves for the roof, because it rains every day.

I had subjects that I was assigned to speak about, as well as offer counseling for the people. I walked with my Bible shut, with the translator for the Dangriga people from southern Belize. There was also Native people that were there, and a big group of youth. So I had to have this translator. The translator's name was Roman, and he was an interesting character. We had fun together. One time I said, "How come it takes you twice as long to say what I said?" He laughed and said, "I guess I forgot to tell you, but I say what you said, and then I say what you meant." Oh, we had fun! That was a good experience.

We slept in a pup tent, Eileen and I. We had our bags in there. My dear wife, she thought the cows were going to tramp all over us in that pup tent! It was a good experience—two weeks out there with these young people, talking with them.

The girls were pretty girls, but they were only 14 and 15 years old. Some of those boys were determined that they wanted to marry one of those girls. They'd come to me and try to get me to set up a wedding for them. The girls would come, and they'd talk to me, too. They'd say, "We don't want to marry them!" I don't know if that ever happened later on or not.

In the evening, people from the German colony would come in and gather in a big banana-leaf-covered pavilion with planks on top of stumps. Probably 200-300 people were there. But the young guys from the German Mennonite colony were wild. During the service they would run their motorcycles through the area, spin their car tires. It was something. And I was to preach. I did!

Not many young fellows, but an awful lot of girls and women in their early 20s would come to me for counseling. Oh my. I don't know, what do you do when you get into another group of people's culture, different religion, different spiritual

John preached and taught at a series of meetings in the German Mennonite colony in Belize in 1985. The primary topic was healthy relationships, and he provided counseling for individuals.

beliefs? These girls wanted to get free of their dads, free from the boys that were down there.

In Canada, there was a conservative Mennonite college, it was called Waterloo something—I can't think of the name of it now. The girls were allowed to go there. I encouraged every one of those girls, "Go there. That might be your gateway to freedom." I often wondered what came out of all of that.

One of my teaching subjects was relationships, boy-girl relationships, male-female relationships. There was a nineteen-year-old young lady who had a high school education. Intelligent, good-looking woman. She was sharp. She'd tell those boys and those men what she thought. She said, "You have the least understanding of what it means to have a good relationship in marriage. You listen to this man."

We would go sometimes during the day out to a lake that they had built there with a big dam. The road was rough, and that truck was not an easy seat, it bounced. One day when we were going out, and I had my arm around Eileen to hold her because of the bouncing, didn't the driver really hit a hole. I went up in the air enough that when I came down on my ribs, I hit the side and I heard them snap. I didn't do any swimming because I couldn't!

We got back to the camp, and I was scheduled to speak. I talked, but I could only give a few words and then I would have to get my breath. It was terrible. It was just so painful. Everybody listened; the boys listened even. They'd never seen anybody, I guess, hurt like that.

They took me to a doctor, a colony doctor. I decided to ask a few questions. I learned he got his education from reading a book! He was considered a doctor, the medical doctor for the whole German colony. He took care of all kinds of things. If it had taken an operation, he wouldn't do an operation, but everything else he'd take care of, births and everything.

He said, "I'd like to examine your chest." So I took my shirt off and laid on a couple planks that had burlap over it. He found them. He said, "You've got some broken ribs. Nothing I can do about that. I'll rub it with liniment for you before you leave." It was like putting fire on my back. I don't know what he had; it was strong stuff! It didn't help.

I had that pain the whole rest of the time I was there. That was an experience of you go to serve, you go to help, and you end up needing help. But that was good. I hope and pray that all the young people that dedicated their lives to the Lord are still growing as Christians. I hope and pray. I think often of the young girls, sure hope they're doing okay.

I wasn't always assigned topics when I was invited to preach. What I came back to over and over again was Jesus Christ and him crucified, risen again, and coming back. I stuck real close to the Gospel. I always did; I still do.

I'd say, "We see pictures of Jesus and his disciples. They look good, very healthy. Good clothing." I said, "But if you really read what Jesus looked like," I said, "he associated with the poor, the sick, the maimed, the lepers, the prostitutes."

You read Isaiah where it says he was despised and rejected, had his beard plucked out. Had stripes on his back that were so severe that he couldn't carry the crossbeam. He did it for me. Sometimes I can make things very vivid by talking. Sometimes I do, and I've been told that they didn't like it. It's too bad. Especially when I would say that Jesus was totally naked on the cross. I've been told about that.

I like to teach. My teaching is broader because usually a church has maybe seven nights or eight nights. Or three nights, or whatever, so I can condense it more. I want people to know that there is hope, there's life, that Jesus meets all that need.

The whole thing that the Bible says, we need to apply that today in today's methodology and way of understanding. It might be different than it was in years past, but we still know what sin is and we still know what salvation is. I don't buy into the idea that some things are for that day and some things are for this day.

I believe the church traditions have a very valuable place. Maybe not the same form of tradition, but traditions are good. They hold communities of people together. They cause a safety net for young couples in their way of looking at each other and thinking about each other as husband and wife. The value of a tradition is that "this is the way we do it."

A lot of the camps I was invited to, it was to talk about relationships. I talk a lot about relationships and how important they are.

Let the work that I've done speak for me

(African-American Spiritual)
Sung by Joe Carter

Let the work that I've done speak for me
Let the work that I've done speak for me
When I come to the end of this road
And I lay down this old heavy load
Let the work that I've done speak for me

Let the life that I've lived speak for me
Let the life that I've lived speak for me
When I come to the end of this road
And I lay down this old heavy load
Let the life that I've lived speak for me

Let the prayers that I've prayed speak for me
Let the prayers that I've prayed speak for me
When I've done the very best that I can
And if my friends don't understand
Let the prayers that I've prayed speak for me

Let the love that I've shared speak for me
Let the love that I've shared speak for me
When I come to the end of this road
And I lay down this old heavy load
Let the life that I've lived speak for me
Let the prayers that I've prayed speak for me
Let the love that I've shared speak for me

Foodways and Fellowship

Eileen: *At home growing up we ate meat and potatoes and potatoes and meat! Ham and beef mostly; we didn't eat much fish. I remember the lettuce salad that my mother would make, and I still make it sometimes. She just made a simple cream dressing and put it on cold lettuce. I enjoyed that.*

My mother made a dish she called Chicken a la King, and she usually made that for company. I really liked that dish. I wish I had the recipe. We always had bread with our meals, and I think we usually had fruit or baked things for dessert—cake probably more than pies.

Breakfast was eggs and cereal. My dad could make soft-boiled eggs, and he would often eat them in the evening before he went to bed. John still remembers of eating soft-boiled eggs with my dad after we came home from a date. John gets a kick out of that.

My parents enjoyed hosting people, and I learned hospitality from them. Even though Mother had her disability in walking, we still had guests. She had quite a few family dinners and close friends, or other friends, who would come. Just like John and I did then. And my dad always had children visiting from Lebanon.

Hosting Hart family (left) and Landis family (right) reunions at the farm.

Each year Eileen and John opened their home to Gingrichs church for a three-day Christmas open house.

Gingrichs Mennonite Church Kitchen Committee, left to right: Kathy Boshart, Alma Landis, Ruth Frey, Eileen Landis, Mabel Weaver, Barb Keener. About 2004.

COMMUNION SERVICE MEAL
Sunday, November 7, 2010

Food	Amount	Leftover
Chicken Noodle Soup	3 gallons	1 Gallon
Vegetable Soup	2 gallons	1 quart
Homemade Bread	4 loaves	Several pieces
Cheese Cubes	5 pounds	½ pound
Crackers, saltines	1 pound box	1/4 lb.
Fresh fruit platters	4 for 8-10 people	½ platter
Butter	1 pound	½ pound
Jelly	1 pint jar	½ jar
Coffee	3 coffee urns	Small amount
Cider	2 gallons	½ gallon
Coffee Creamer	1 quart	1 pint

34 persons attended including 4 small children

We used 2 cookers for heating soup. We put all the food on the tables so we could concentrate on Scriptures and discussion at the tables.

John: I am glad for the wife that I have. We decided early on that we would follow her parents' example of inviting people out to our farm.

We love people. We always developed relationships with people. I always had a pick up truck, or a little flat bed, and I moved so many people. People that couldn't pay anybody to move them, I would move them.

For a while I worked with Jubilee in helping people with their finances. I helped so many people pay off their debts, just by changing the management of their finances. I confronted a couple of individuals in business. They got the message. These rental companies for furniture, they are terrible.

But yes, we have a heart for people.

"I am glad for the wife that I have."

Eileen: *We did have lots of people coming and going. I accept people for what they are. Let them join in with whatever is going on.*

Each year we had a picnic for Gingrichs church in our yard. We did that for years and years. At Christmas time we had a four-day Christmas open house! We had a Landis family picnic every year.

John: It's been fun. It's been a blessing.

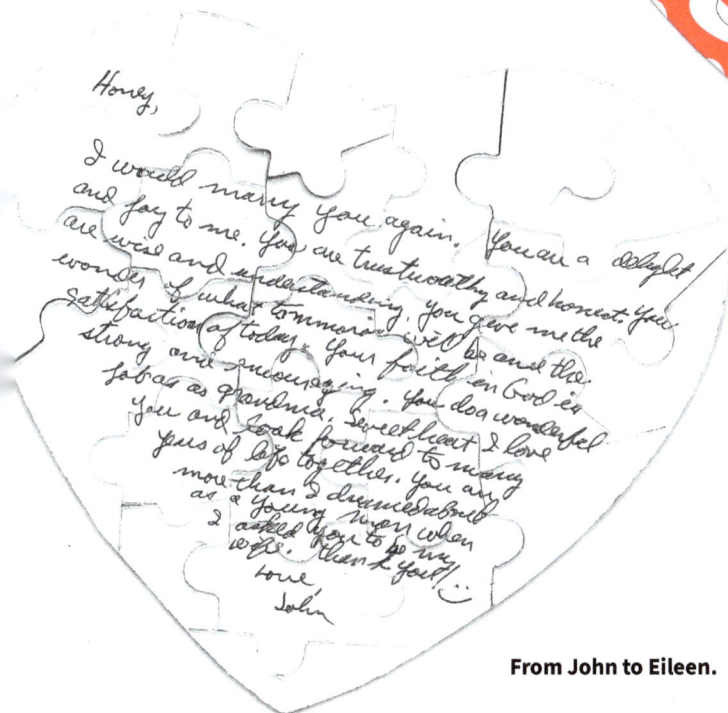

From John to Eileen.

Tidbits and Other Stories

John: When I was growing up at Landis Valley Mennonite Church, there were 13 John Landises. How did they keep us separate? Well, most of those John Landises were married. So when they wanted to talk about Emma's John, it was Emma's John; it was Sally's John, Helen's John. They always put the wife's name in front of the John Landis. Catherine's John.

Which I thought was kind of neat that the women were not excluded; they were very much a part of the Landis family system. My grandpa and grandma were identified a lot of times as Anna Mary and John. I liked that. That was good. You gotta have something that you can be guided by. You got 13 John Landises, it's like having a bunch of Stoltzfuses or Riehls or somebody else, like in the Amish. Sometimes they talk about it, that it's hard to identify who's who.

• • • • •

Eileen: *It's an interesting time of life right now. Our children are all grown, they're in their fifties. It's interesting to see how they have taken ideas, like just a simple one: we always had sticky buns and hot chocolate on Christmas morning, and most of them still do that.*

We encourage them. Sometimes it's hard to keep our mouth shut when we think they're making a wrong decision. And yet, I thought, it was probably hard for our parents to keep quiet. They didn't tell us what to do.

• • • • •

John: Pop and Mom wanted me to be separated from the world. That was a term that was used a lot by pastors. I always struggled with that. I didn't wear any plain clothes until I was a junior or senior at LMH. I always wore a tie.

But there comes those times that you make decisions, and they can bring heartaches in families. It did for me. When I was either a sophomore or junior at LMH

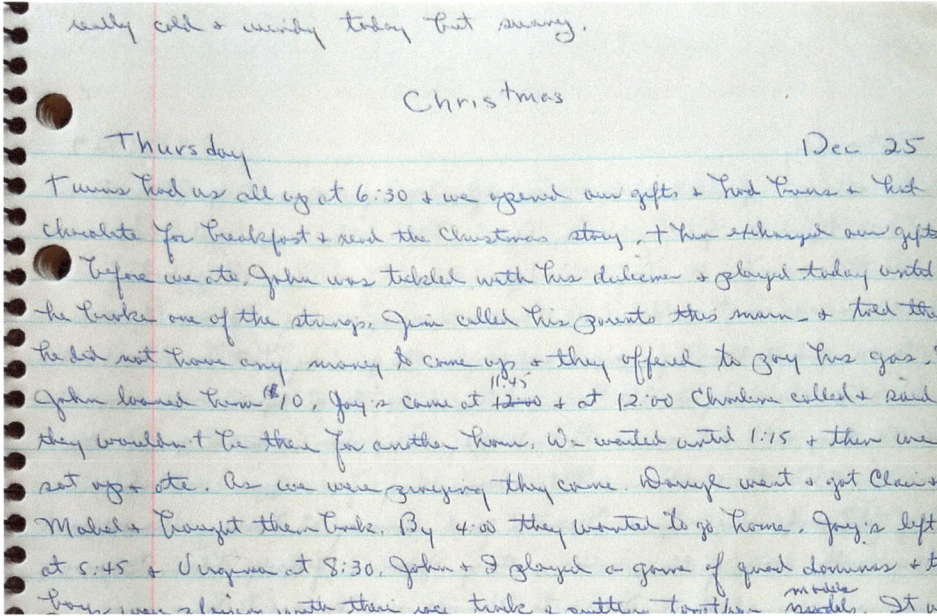

A Christmas morning, as recorded by Eileen in her diary. Year circa early 80s.

I got a crew haircut, cut short and blocky. I can still see my mother crying when I came home from the barber. That I didn't want; that I didn't like.

When I quit wearing my plain suit, I went to my mother and talked to her. Pop was no longer living at that time. Mother had switched from "being separated from the world" to "You're a pastor. You should be wearing a plain suit." Yet she realized that I was a full-grown man with children and that she couldn't tell me what to do. So she left it up to me. She said, "If you want to not wear a plain suit, I won't stop you. I won't say any more from here on out. That's your decision."

"But," she said, "if you made a vow that you're going to wear a plain suit to be pastor, I think you need to keep it." I checked into that: I had not said that I would continue wearing a plain suit as a pastor. So she accepted that.

That was good; it was a tough time. I never liked going against my mother.

• • • • •

When I was a travelling evangelist, I got into a lot of churches and homes. As an outside person, pastors felt comfortable telling me their struggles. "Who's in charge?" was the biggest problem I found among the pastors in the up to 200 churches I was in.

• • • • •

Singing would begin a half hour to an hour before revival meetings. Song leaders from different congregations would be there. One song leader would walk to the front and announce who would lead the next song before leading. My brother, Mark, might go to the front and say "John Landis is going to lead the next song." When his song is done, I walk up and say "So-and-so is going to lead the next song," and I'd lead the one I chose.

• • • • •

As pastor, I performed more than 300 weddings.

• • • • •

I'm a person that often tried different recipes. I liked to try new things, and then I'd forget about it!

• • • • •

Throughout life I found I'd rather be in the background, supporting John, giving him ideas. There were times I gave him ideas, and he implemented them. That's fine with me. I enjoy that role in life.

• • • • •

Raymond Charles gave me this on the topic of "Who are the Mennonites?"

B —Believers baptism
A —Authority of the Scriptures
S —Separation from the world
I —Involvement of the brotherhood
N —Nonresistance

I used to use it when I taught about the Mennonites one day a year for 15 years in Cedar Crest junior and senior humanities classes.

Crowd-sized Recipes

From Eileen Landis' recipe collection for serving large groups

A Recipe for **Broccoli Turkey Salad**   10 servings

Ingredients   1 can 8 oz. Pineapple chunks, Drained
2 cups Torn Salad greens
2 cups Torn Fresh Spinach   Combine
2 cups Broccoli Florts   Together
1 green pepper, julienned
½ cup thinly sliced onion
2 cups cubed cooked Turkey

Combine in small bowl
¼ cup olive or vegetable oil   2 tsp. Sugar
2 TBlSP balsamic vinger or redwine vinegar   2 Tsp Dijon mustard
1 TBLSP Poppy Seeds   2 TBlSP Pineapple Juice
Pour over salad + toss to coat. Serve immediately

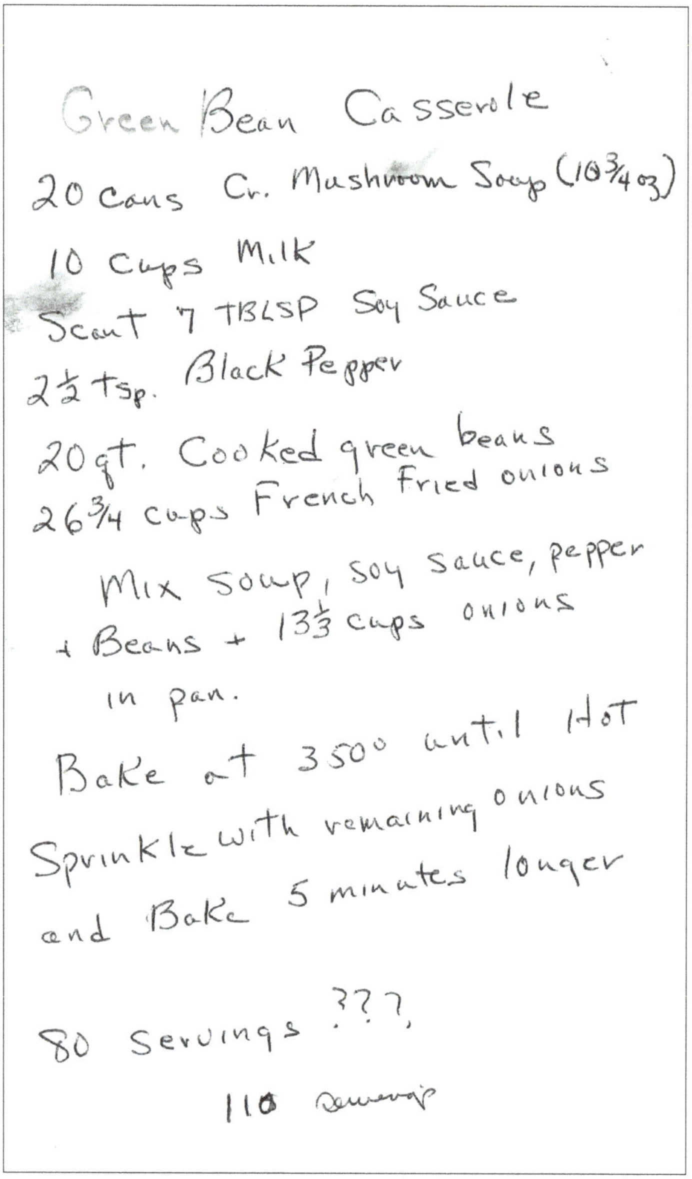

Green Bean Casserole

20 cans Cr. Mushroom Soup (10¾ oz)

10 cups Milk

Scant 7 TBLSP Soy Sauce

2½ tsp. Black Pepper

20 qt. Cooked green beans

26¾ cups French Fried onions

Mix Soup, Soy Sauce, pepper
+ Beans + 13⅓ cups onions
in pan.

Bake at 350° until Hot
Sprinkle with remaining onions
and Bake 5 minutes longer

80 Servings ???,

110 servings

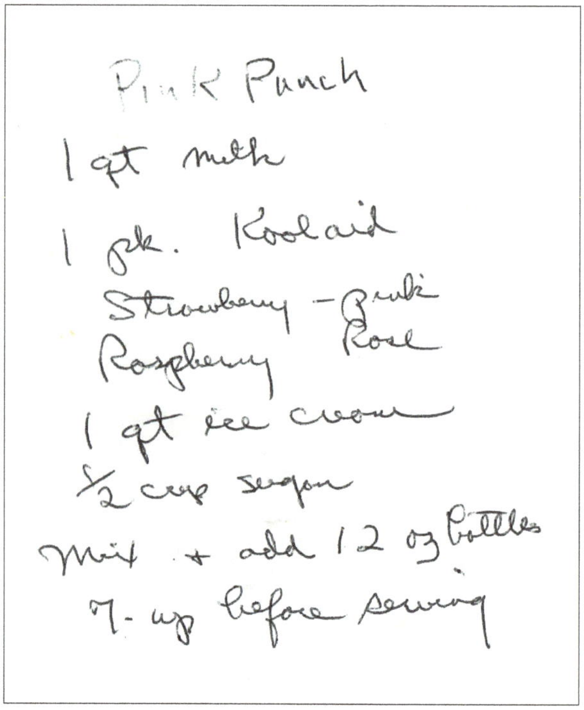

Pink Punch

1 qt milk

1 pk. Koolaid
    Strawberry — pink
    Raspberry   Rose

1 qt ice cream

½ cup sugar

Mix + add 12 oz bottles
   7-up before serving

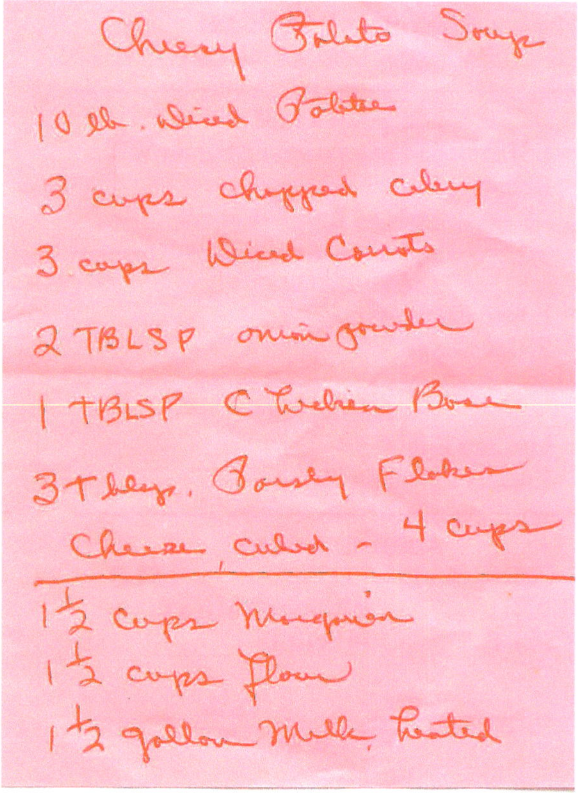

Cheesy Potato Soup

10 lb. Diced Potatoes

3 cups chopped celery

3 cups Diced Carrots

2 TBLSP onion powder

1 TBLSP Chicken Base

3 Tbsp. Parsley Flakes

Cheese, cubed — 4 cups

1½ cups Margarine

1½ cups flour

1½ gallon Milk, heated

Chicken a la King

Ingredients	per 12	ser 25	ser 50	ser 100
Margarine	7/8 c	1 3/4 c	1 3/4 #	3 1/2 #
Flour	1 c	2 c	4 c	8 c
Chicken stock, hot	3 cups	1 1/2 qt	3 1/4 qt	6 1/2 qt
Salt – optional or adjust	1 1/2 tsp	1 tbsp	2 tbsp	4 tbsp
White Pepper, adjust	dash	1/8 tsp	1/4 tsp	1/2 tsp
Milk, hot	2 c	1 qt	2 qt	4 qt
chicken, cooked, boned & cubed	1 1/4 #	2 1/2 #	5 #	10 #
Eggs hard cooked, chopped	3	1/2 doz	1 doz	2 doz
Pimento, chopped or shredded	1/3 c	3/4 cup	1 1/4 c	2 1/2 c
Mushrooms, canned & drained	1/4 c	1/2 c	1 c	2 c
Green peppers, shredded or diced thin strips, cooked) or substitute	1/3 c	3/4 cup	1 1/2 c	3 c
Peas, frozen, cooked	1/3 c	3/4 cup	1 1/2 c	3 c

portion

Method 200

1. Melt marg.; add flour stir until smooth. Add salt if used.
2. Add hot chicken broth & milk gradually, stirring constantly
3. Cook & stir as necessary until smooth & thick (22 min)
4. Add rest of ingredients & heat through – do not boil
5. Serve over toast, waffles cornbread or rice

HAMBURGER-MACARONI CASSEROLE

INGREDIENTS	PORTIONS 10-12	25	50
Hamburger, browned	2 1/2 lb	5 lbs	10 lbs
Onion powder	2 Tsp	1 TBLSP	2 TBLSP
Macaroni	2 1/2 cups	5 Cups	10 Cups
Cheese, Velveeta	3/4 lb.	1 1/2 lb	3 lbs
Tomato soup, 51 oz. can	1/2 can	1	2 (51 oz)

METHOD

1. Brown hamburger and add . onion powder
2. Cook cups of macaroni and add to browned macaroni
3. Add . Velveeta Cheese, cut in small pieces. Add can tomato soup. If more liquid is needed use tomato juice.

Bake approximately 1 - 1 1/2 hours in 350° oven

Place in counter pan.

Gallery

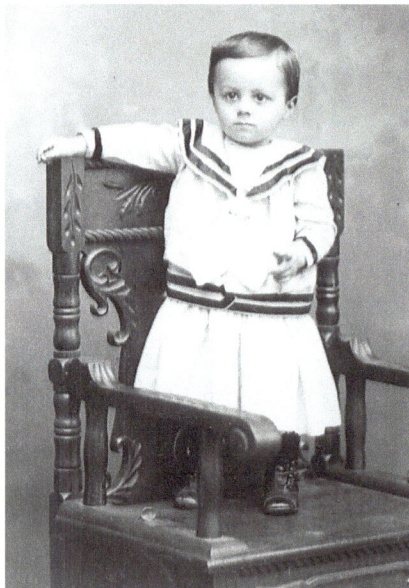

John's father, Elam Landis, born September 15, 1906.

John's parents and grandparents, celebrating his parents' 25th wedding anniversary on December 31, 1956. Left to right: John L. Landis, Anna Mary Oberholtzer Landis, Elam O. Landis, Ruth F. Garman Landis, Katie Frey Garman, Frank Garman.

Quartet practice circa 1964. Left to right: John Landis with Darryl at his knee, and three Boll brothers: Lester, Elvin, and Homer. John sang bass, Elvin was first tenor, Lester second tenor, and Homer baritone. John says, "During that time we all had little children. We'd talk and watch the children while we practiced. It was a very good time for us as young couples." The quartet, called Boll Brothers and John Landis, did many programs in churches and sang at weddings—almost every weekend for a period of time. A CD recording of this quartet exists.

John became a board member of Lancaster Mennonite Historical Society in April 1969, shortly after the Society began and moved into this, its new building at 2215 Millstream Road, Lancaster.

March 24, 1969

MENNONITE INFORMATION CENTER
LIBRARY & ARCHIVES
2215 Mill Stream Rd.
Lincoln Hgwy., East U. S. Rt. 30
Lancaster, Penna.
Ph. 717 - 397-7811
Open Monday Thru Sat. 9:00 to 5:00

Dear Bro. John:

You have been informed, and will soon be officially, that you have been appointed to serve as a member of our historical society. Your first meeting will be Monday evening, April 14, at our library. I trust that you will be able to be present. We are looking forward to your contribution in the days ahead.

Fraternally,

Ira D. Landis

Post Card

Mr. John G. Landis

Route 4

Lebanon, Pennsylvania 17042

Ernest Weinhold, left, and John Landis, right, in the Lancaster Mennonite Historical Society library.

A project of the Lancaster Mennonite Historical Society, John served on the committee that restored the 1719 Herr House in the late 1970s and registered it on the National Register of Historic Places. He said, "Oh the arguments we had! Arguments about why we should restore the Herr House. 'Let the township or someone else restore it,' some said. We considered it an outreach." The house and museum are located at 1849 Hans Herr Drive, Willow Street, PA. Archeological digs at the site have taken place over the years.

John addressing the Lancaster Mennonite School graduating class of 1986.

In memory of
ELAM O. LANDIS

Born September 15, 1906

Entered into rest November 10, 1977

Services, Monday, November 14, 1977

10:00 o'clock

Landis Valley Mennonite Church

Officiating Clergy
Elam Stauffer
Lester Hoover
Ervin Weaver
John G. Landis
John A. Lutz

Interment in Adjoining Cemetery

Pallbearers

Melvin Bauman	Jeffrey Landis
Timothy Landis	Keith Landis
Thomas Landis	David Lutz
Daryl Landis	Jerry Bauman

FURMAN HOME FOR FUNERALS — LEOLA, PENNSYLVANIA

In memory of

Ruth F. Landis

Born October 14, 1910
Entered into rest February 28, 1998

Services Wednesday March 4, 1998
Ten o'clock in the morning

Landis Valley Mennonite Church

Interment in the adjacent cemetery

Officiating Clergy

Tom Horst	Don Good
Paul Weaver	John G. Landis

Pallbearers

Melvin Bauman	Tom Landis
Darryl Landis	David Lutz
Mark Nissley	Frank Cicero Jr.
Abigail Landis	

Furman Home for Funerals Leola, Pa.

John had the honor of being among the officiating ministers at each of his parents' funerals.

John says: My dad made a clock for Mom and someone said, "It would be nice if you'd make one for each of your children." So in '77 he had made all the children a clock and had them all over at the neighbors. He was going to give them as gifts at Christmas, and he died in November. After the funeral we were all at Mom's place with her, and she said "There's one more thing before anybody goes. I have something I want to show you, but it's over at the neighbors." None of us had a clue. We walked across the yard to the neighbors, and there, along one wall, was seven grandfather clocks, all running. I'll never forget that. We said, "Pop will speak to us every hour, every 15 minutes!"

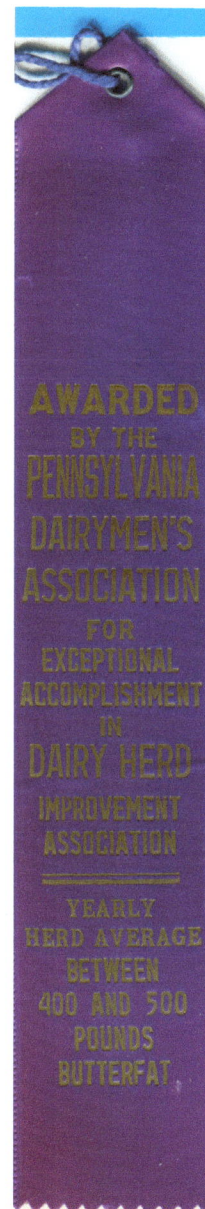

Dairy award, 1959.

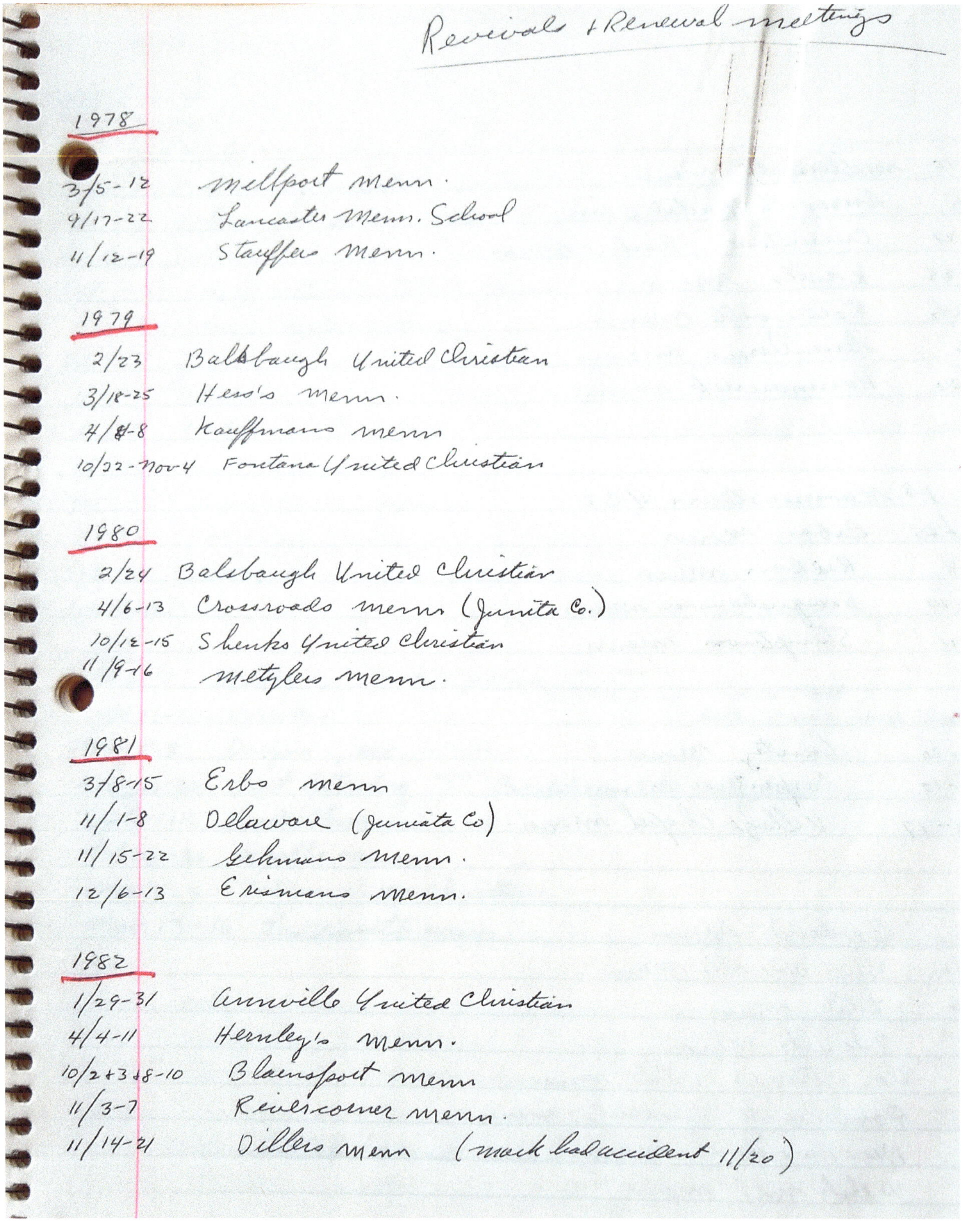

Revivals + Renewal meetings

1978

3/5-12   Millport Menn.
4/17-22   Lancaster Menn. School
11/12-19   Stauffers Menn.

1979

2/23   Balsbaugh United Christian
3/18-25   Hess's Menn.
4/8-8   Kauffmans menn
10/22-Nov4   Fontana United Christian

1980

2/24   Balsbaugh United Christian
4/6-13   Crossroads menn (Juniata Co.)
10/12-15   Shenks United Christian
11/9-16   Metzlers Menn.

1981

3/8-15   Erbs menn
11/1-8   Delaware (Juniata Co)
11/15-22   Gehmans Menn.
12/6-13   Erismans menn.

1982

1/29-31   Annville United Christian
4/4-11   Hernley's Menn.
10/2+3+8-10   Blainsport menn
11/3-7   Rivercorner menn.
11/14-21   Dillers menn   (mack had accident 11/20)

1988

Jan.-Feb. Winter Bible School, Andrew Bridge, Cedar Hill, Hammercreek, Dillers, Buffaloe
        Lost creek   "Children in Worship"
Jan.-Feb. Jubilee ministries - Parenting classes = (10)
Jan.24   Laurel St. Lanc. Pa. "Law & Grace"
Feb. 7   Lincoln University - "Evangelism" - P.m.
   13   Hammercreek M.Y.F. Sweetheart bang. -
   20   United Christian Manada Gap Sweet heart bang.
Mar.18-20 Black Rock Retreat - Cedar Grove Young couples = "Parenting"
Apr. 1   Kauffmans Y.M. Methodist - My God, My God, why have you forsaken me?
   18   Cedar crest = "Who are the mennonites"
   30   Hebron mann church, MD. (A.C.C. conf. on leadership)
May 28   Juniata Dist - subject = Prayer.
June 7, 13, +20 - Millwood = Training counselors for Tent meeting   steps to Peace
June 12 - Fairland Bic · Youth groups
June 19 - Carpenters menn. = "Being Dad in Family"
July 6, 7, 8, 9 = United Zion Camp meeting - Study of Book of Phil.
July 23 - 29 = Camp Hebron = teach
aug. 7 Maple Grove M.Y.F. = Peace + Non - Resistance
aug. 8+9 = Baltimore YES = How to Study the Bible Inductively
aug. 13 = Cove Valley Family Camp. = The Dynamics of Family
aug. 17 = United Christian Camp meeting = "The Be's Nest" Eph. 5:
Sept. 15 = L.M.H. Chapel
Sept. 17 = Camp Andrews
Sept. 21 ,28 Oct 5 +12 = Adult Ed. · Children in Worship
Nov. 12 = Lanc. Conf. Youth Leaders Festival
Dec. 31 = Fairland Youth - Watch night

A sampling of the speaking and counseling schedules John kept, while also farming and pastoring with his family's help and support.

1997
7-12   missie + Rodney Bomgardner
10-25   Rick + Chrissy Gomer
6-7   Kathy Bomgardner + Kent Martin   - meditation

1998
Sept. 19   Bry Ebersole + Jen Balsbour - counsel + wed.

<u>1999</u>
May 1   Dawson + Jody Hostetter - counseling + wed.
May 29   Pret + Rhonda Zook   - "   "   "
June 12   Kent + Melonica Hoffer   - "   "   "
July 2   Greg + Katie Bomgardner   - "   "   "
August 21   David + Jane Baffenmoyer   -   "
August 28   Jon + Markay Freed   - "   "   "
Sept. 3   Scott + Angie Billman   - "   "   "
Sept. 25   Larry + Tricia Kreider   - "   "   "
Oct. 9   Brian + Karlene Bean   - "   "   "
Oct. 16   Tim   + Yemi Hailesellasi   "

2000
Aug 12   Sarah + Andrew - counseling + wedding
Sept. 24   Ryan + Beth (Freed) Umble · counsel + wed.

2001
May 27   - Carla Hart + Tony Hertzler = counsel + marry
June 2   - Todd Hartman + Kim   = counsel + marry

A GREATER LOVE
John 15:1-17

I. Intro: Setting and context

- Passover
- Cup & bread
- wash the Disciples feet
- Disciples/who is the greatest - Lk 22:24-30
- Peter's denial foretold
- Jesus tells of his going away
- Promise of the Holy Spirit given
- Now leaving the upper room
- Shows "GOD IS LOVE" & our connection to this love

II. LOVE ENLARGES OUR RELATIONSHIP == fruit
- Connected to the Vine, have the life of the Vine & so the fruit of the Vine
   A. Giving us His Attributes
      - God's love & character to others
         - God, Jesus life in us.   - meet People
         - the nature of God   -
            - born of God

   B. Changing our attitudes   - Big bumbling Peter
      - Self denial versus Pride   - Sons of thunder
      - servant hood versus Boss   - Tax collector
      - live for good of others versus myself   zealot
      - unselfishness / versus greed
      - Peace maker & forgiveness versus conflict + bitterness
      - death so we live versus living so we don't die

   C. expressing our actions
      - I will be touched
      - I will touch
                                        - be good Samaritans
         - relatively   - heal People
         - consistently   -
         - cooperatively

   Illus = Jan Saver coal

John's sermon notes from "A Greater Love," a favorite sermon of his son Darryl.

2

III. LOVE ENABLES OUR WORTH == fruition

A. Feeling Significant = *people of God*
  - loved   *kingdom of Christ*
  - I am important
  - *as Father loves me, So, I love you.*
  - *From a nobody to God's Chosen*

B. Having Security   *= I'll always be with you*
  - remain   *- my kingdom not of this world*
  - Accepted
  - non-threatening
  - A place I want to come, to be
  - cherished, honored, protected

C. Being Sensual   *- Joy not based on a*
  - Complete Joy   *- good cates of feel*
  - Feeling of worth *- Percentage of income*
  - *a sense of meekness*   *- Purifying*

illus = Abby with

IV. LOVE ENSURES OUR POSITION == friends
                    - I have chosen you
A. Freedom Given
  - Chosen while a slave
  - *relieved of bondage of being a slave*
  - *Redemption = Purchased from slave mkt.*
  - *to become all that I can, am designed to become*
  - *One same love that changed us and gave us a new relationship and worth ...... guarantees our position*

3.

B. Friendship Established
- "I tell you"
- Open understanding
- Free interaction/ give & take
- In on the planning

C. Family Acceptance
- "Ask the Father"
- The resources of Heaven
- God is an accepting Father
    - Arms wide open to receive us
- Jesus is our older (elder) brother

Illust: Jim Perkins
Martin Luther King

V. HOW CAN THIS BE?

A. A Greater Love = God's love goes beyond feeling - to will & thought/choice

B. I lay down My Life = a sacrificial love that that gives itself for others

C. Jesus did this for us. Later that Day Jesus was crucified.
- lived
- died
- rose again
- at work for us - intercessor
- coming again

A gift from the Krall's Mennonite Church congregation in 2015 when John and Eileen completed their eight years of pastoral service there.

Service honoring and concluding Landises' 23-year pastoral leadership at Gingrichs Mennonite Church. Here Eileen looks on while John passes a symbol of leadership to Rick and Sarah Conrad, the incoming pastoral couple.

Eileen and friends enjoying Seniors Camp at Camp Hebron, Halifax, PA.

Pastor John's Daily Prayer from Scripture

I am crucified with Christ:
nevertheless I live;
yet not I, but Christ liveth in me:
and the life which I now live in the flesh
I live by the faith of the Son of God,
who loved me, and gave himself for me.

But God forbid that I should glory,
save in the cross of our Lord Jesus Christ,
by whom the world is crucified unto me,
and I unto the world.

And this I pray,
That your love may abound yet more and more
in knowledge and in all judgment;
That you may approve things that are excellent;
that you may be sincere and without offence
till the day of Christ;
Being filled with the fruits of righteousness,
which are by Jesus Christ, unto the glory and praise of God.

Galatians 2:20 and 6:14, Philippians 1:9-11

1 I owe the Lord a morn-ing song Of grat - i - tude and praise,
2 He kept me safe an - oth - er night; I see an - oth - er day;
3 Keep me from dan - ger and from sin: Help me Thy will to do,
4 Keep me till Thou wilt call me hence, Where nev - er night can be;

For the kind mer - cy He has shown In length-'ning out my days.
Now may His Spir - it, as the light, Di - rect me in His way.
So that my heart be pure with-in; And I Thy good-ness know.
And save me, Lord, for Je - sus' sake. He shed His blood for me. A-men.

A prayer and song John shared through his chaplain work at Countryside Christian Community. *Artwork by Christina Okamoto*

John served as chaplain at Countryside Christian Community, a retirement home in Annville, from 2007 to 2019. Here he checks in with residents.

Dear

I have decided to send each of you a blank tablet for your January gift for several reasons. January is the first month of a new year 2005. I am thinking of each day in this new year as a bunch of blank pages. You will have the opportunity to fill your blank days with deeds that are kind, loving and worthwhile or just goof around and do things that will not be very good and fulfilling when you come to the end of 2005.

You may use this book for anything that you want to ---maybe homework assignments --maybe a diary –(this is the kind of notebook I use for my yearly dairy) --maybe someplace to doodle –or you could use it as writing paper for notes to friends --or anything else that you might need paper for. Just try to remember what the pages mean and fill your lives with the best that you can this year.

Love,

Love Blank Notebooks
January 2005

Since many of their grandchildren lived far away, up until each one was about age 10 Eileen and John would send a monthly note. Here's one from January 2005.

Sent to Grandchildren   Oct. 2002

THIS PUZZLE WILL TELL YOU WHAT YOUR GRANDPARENTS THINK OF YOU!

1.　　　　　W __ __ __ __ __ __ __ __

2.　　__ __ E__ __ __ __ __

3.　　__ __ L__ __

4.　　　__O__ __ __

5.　　　V__ __ __ __ __

6.　　__ __ E__ __ __ __

7. __ __ __ Y

8. __ __ __ O__ __ __ __ __ __

9. __ __ __ U__

ANSWERS

1. We think you are _____ and great grandchildren

2. You grandchildren are _____ to us.

3. We _____ you very much.

4. God _____ each of us.

5. We look forward to your _____.

6. You are _____ to us.

7. We _____ for you each day.

8. Each of you are _____ persons to us.

9. We are _____ you are our grandchildren.

Sent with puzzle

I am sending you a game
That will work the Brain.
So grab your pencil or pen
And try to Finish before ten.
I don't want you to lose Sleep.

More examples of fun and creative things Eileen and John sent to grandchildren.

SCHOOL
by Grandma

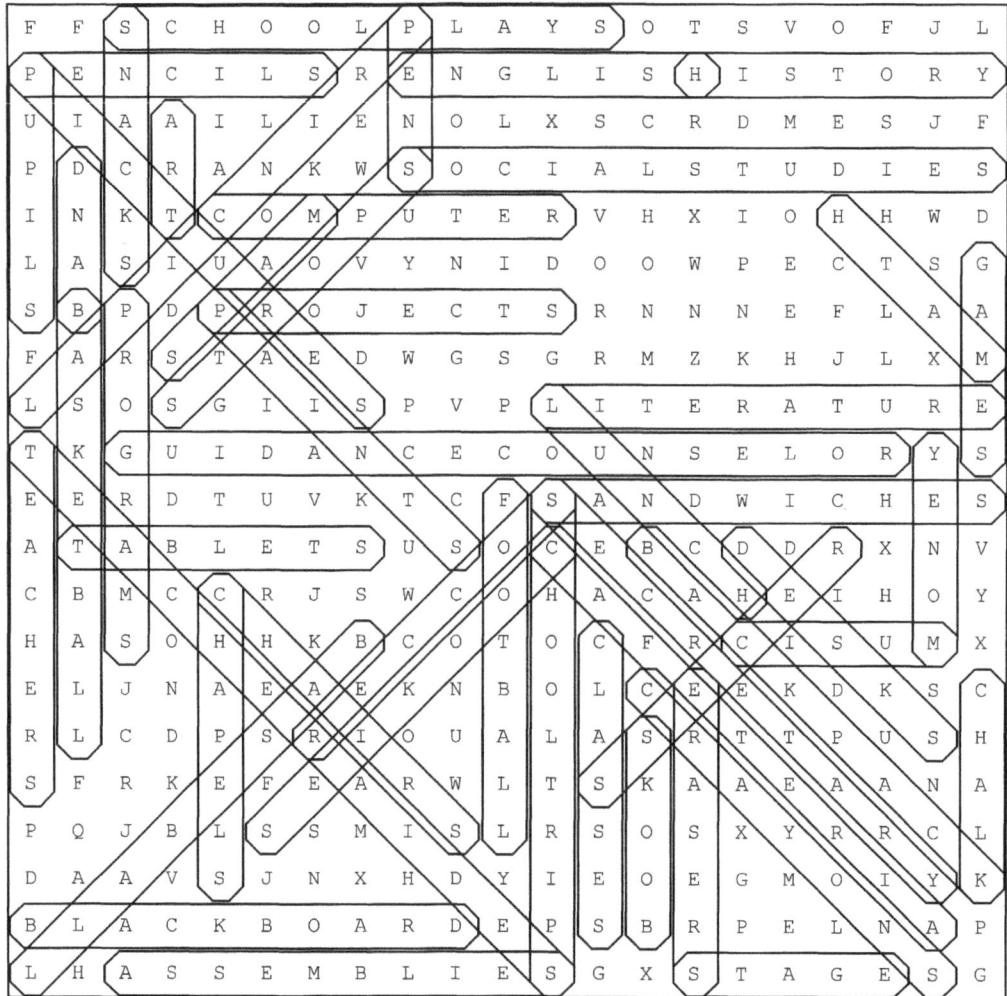

```
F  F  S  C  H  O  O  L  P  L  A  Y  S  O  T  S  V  O  F  J  L
P  E  N  C  I  L  S  R  E  N  G  L  I  S  H  I  S  T  O  R  Y
U  I  A  I  L  I  E  N  O  L  X  S  C  R  D  M  E  S  J  F
P  D  C  R  A  N  K  W  S  O  C  I  A  L  S  T  U  D  I  E  S
I  N  K  T  C  O  M  P  U  T  E  R  V  H  X  I  O  H  H  W  D
L  A  S  I  U  A  O  V  Y  N  I  D  O  O  W  P  E  C  T  S  G
S  B  P  D  P  R  O  J  E  C  T  S  R  N  N  N  E  F  L  A  A
F  A  R  S  T  A  E  D  W  G  S  G  R  M  Z  K  H  J  L  X  M
L  S  O  G  I  I  S  P  V  P  L  I  T  E  R  A  T  U  R  E  E
T  K  G  U  I  D  A  N  C  E  C  O  U  N  S  E  L  O  R  Y  S
E  E  R  D  T  U  V  K  T  C  F  S  A  N  D  W  I  C  H  E  S
A  T  B  M  C  C  R  J  S  W  C  O  C  E  B  C  D  D  R  X  N  V
C  B  M  C  C  R  J  S  W  C  O  H  A  C  A  H  E  I  H  O  Y
H  A  S  O  H  H  K  B  C  O  T  O  C  F  R  C  I  S  U  M  X
E  L  J  N  A  E  A  E  K  N  B  O  L  C  E  E  K  D  K  S  C
R  L  C  D  P  S  R  I  O  U  A  L  A  S  R  T  T  P  U  S  H
S  F  R  K  E  F  E  A  R  W  L  T  S  K  A  A  E  A  N  A
P  Q  J  B  L  S  S  M  I  S  L  R  S  O  S  X  Y  R  R  C  L
D  A  A  V  S  J  N  X  H  D  Y  I  E  O  E  G  M  O  I  Y  K
B  L  A  C  K  B  O  A  R  D  E  P  S  B  R  P  E  L  N  A  P
L  H  A  S  S  E  M  B  L  I  E  S  G  X  S  T  A  G  E  S  G
```

Sep 4, 2002

Word List

ART
ASSEMBLIES
BACKPACK
BAND
BASEBALL
BASKETBALL
BLACKBOARD
BOOKS
CAFETERIA
CHAIRS
CHALK
CHAPELS
CLASSES
COMPUTER
COOKIES
CRAYONS
DESKS
ENGLISH

ERASERS
FOOTBALL
GAMES
GUIDANCECOUNSELOR
HISTORY
LITERATURE
LUNCH
MAPS
MATH
MONEY
MUSIC
PAINTS
PENCILS
PENS
PICTURES
PRINCIPAL
PROGRAMS
PROJECTS
PUPILS
RECESS

SANDWICHES
SCHOOLPLAYS
SCHOOLTRIPS
SECRETARY
SNACKS
SOCCER
SOCIALSTUDIES
SPORTS
STAGE
TABLETS
TEACHERAIDES
TEACHERS

Genealogy

Eileen M. Hart Landis' Parents, Grandparents, and Great-grandparents

Sarah Hershey
b. January 18, 1860
d. August 28, 1944

Levi Wenger
b. September 11, 1861
d. September 13, 1926

Margaret Wenger
b. August 13, 1883
d. May 3, 1961

Lydia Groff
b. February 7, 1839
d. February 4, 1901

Jacob Kreider
b. February 13, 1841
d. July 20, 1908

Willis Groff Kreider
b. August 28, 1881
d. May 3, 1943

(Mary) Elizabeth Kreider
b. April 19, 1914
d. July 23, 2001

Barbara Graybill Snyder
b. June 16, 1850
d. February 19, 1897
Jacob's 2nd wife:
Leah Kauffman
b. Sep. 6, 1860;
d. July 2, 1944

Jacob Winey Benner
b. April 17, 1851
d. February 15, 1917

Annie Benner
b. August 18, 1880
d. May 14, 1960

Eileen Marie Hart Landis
b. May 2, 1937

Susannah Smith
b. October 11, 1845
d. October 31, 1903

Henry S. Hart
b. July 1, 1832
d. September 22, 1914

Edward Dervin Hart
b. August 2, 1879
d. July 17, 1959

Jacob Henry Hart
b. August 2, 1910
d. May 19, 1961

John G. Landis' Parents, Grandparents, and Great-grandparents

Emma Lehn

Katie Frey
b. February 24, 1888
d. January 14, 1979

Jacob Frey
b. August 19, 1858
d. September 25, 1914

Ruth Frey Garman
b. October 14, 1910
d. February 28, 1998

Sarah Kulp (?)

Frank Garman
b. November 26, 1886
d. July 23, 1970

Benjamin Garman
b. April 21, 1853
d.

John Garman Landis
b. March 19, 1937

Lydia Weaver
b. June 12, 1845
d. October 30, 1914

Anna Mary Oberholtzer
b. May 5, 1876
d. May 17, 1962

Christian H. Oberholtzer
b. May 11, 1837
d. February 17, 1920

Elam Oberholtzer Landis
b. September 15, 1906
d. November 10, 1977

Susan Landis
b. June 23, 1833
d. January 28, 1900

John Landis Landis
b. March 19, 1873
d. January 16, 1960

Isaac Landis
b. April 14, 1823
d. February 11, 1897

John & Eileen's Children, Grandchildren, Great-grandchildren

John Garman Landis, born March 19, 1937, and Eileen Marie Hart, born May 2, 1937, married December 28, 1957.

1. Darryl Lynn Landis, b. August 21, 1962
2. Keith Lamar Landis, b. June 26, 1964
3. Rose Ann Landis, b. April 21, 1965
4. Dwight Elam Landis, b. February 19, 1968
5. Dwayne Jacob Landis, b. February 19, 1968
6. James Joseph Peshina (foster son), b. May 28, 1961

Darryl Lynn Landis was married June 27, 1987 to Georgette Stefanie Rosse (b. October 3, 1954, d. November 30, 1988, buried in Gingrichs Mennonite Cemetery.)

1. Darryl John Landis, b. March 7, 1988, d. March 8, 1988, buried in Gingrichs Mennonite Cemetery

Darryl Lynn Landis was married June 8, 1991 to Suhaila Abu Sheacha (b. February 14, 1959.)

2. Abdulla John Landis, b. January 9, 1992
3. Michael Ibrahim Landis, b. August 4, 1993
4. Justin Tawfik Landis, b. March 14, 1995

Keith Lamar Landis was married May 11, 1991 to Brenda Kay Yoder (b. July 27, 1968.)

1. Amber Nicole Landis, b. July 10, 1994
2. Sarah Rose Landis, b. June 15, 1996
3. Andrew Keith Landis, b. March 2, 1999

Rose Ann Landis was married May 22, 1988 to Gerald Robert Baer (b. September 9, 1954.)

1. Michael Baer, b. December 13, 1989
2. Christine Rose Baer, b. October 16, 1991
3. Anne Marie Baer, b. November 19, 1993, married June 12, 2016 to Eric Logan Kemp (b. February 25, 1993.)
   a. Ellamae Rose Kemp, b. July 15, 2019

Dwight Elam Landis was married May 9, 1992 to Gwendolyn Kay Peachey (b. September 30, 1969.)

1. Benjamin Dwayne Landis, b. April 9, 1995, married June 22, 2019 to Morgan Ann Balsbaugh (b. May 28, 1994.)

2. Jacob Gregory Landis, b. March 29, 1997, married June 13, 2020 to Meghan Lysle Hamilton (b. March 6, 1997.)

3. Zachary Dwight Landis, b. March 18, 1999

Dwayne Jacob Landis was married July 25, 1987 to Corlene Sue Beachy (b. July 18, 1968.)

1. Kendall Dwight Landis, b. March 22, 1989, married December 31, 2011 to Julie Jyl Weaver (b. July 11, 1990.)

    a. Jackson Cole Landis, b. September 20, 2015

    b. Braxton James Landis, b. December 21, 2018

2. Stephen Matthew Landis, b. September 11, 1991, married June 30, 2018 to Uri Azareel Rebolledo (b. September 30, 1993.)

James Joseph Peshina, recently known as James Kofalt, was married August 20, 1983 to Ruth Ellen Miller (b. February 6, 1960.)

1. Elya Mae Peshina, b. October 21, 1984, married August 12, 2006 to Braden Marc Brubaker (b. November 4, 1984.)

    a. Alexis Joy Brubaker, b. December 24, 2011

    b. Nicholas Scott Brubaker, b. February 27, 2015

2. Destiny Joy Peshina, b. February 12, 1986, d. June 15, 2020, married June 6, 2009 to Christopher Higdon (b. August 20, 1983.)

3. Ryan Jay Peshina, b. August 19, 1987

    a. Kashton Lee Peshina, b. September 11, 2012

www.ingramcontent.com/pod-product-compliance
Lightning Source LLC
Chambersburg PA
CBHW040735150426

42811CB00063B/1637